1066

1066
THE LOST HASTINGS BATTLEFIELD

DAVID BARNBY

Pen & Sword
MILITARY

AN IMPRINT OF PEN & SWORD BOOKS LTD.
YORKSHIRE – PHILADELPHIA

First published in Great Britain in 2023 by
PEN AND SWORD MILITARY
An imprint of
Pen & Sword Books Limited
Yorkshire – Philadelphia

Port of Hastings illustration by John Tucker
and maps by John Leftwich

Copyright © David Barnby, 2023

ISBN 978 1 39904 905 4

David Barnby has asserted his right to be identified as the author of this Work in accordance with Copyright, Design and Patent Act 1988.

All rights reserved. No part of this book may be reproduced, stored in a retrieval system or transmitted, in any form or by any means, without the written permission of the author.

Whilst every effort has been made to trace the copyright holders of anything used in this book, if the author has inadvertently overlooked any publishers, he would be glad to hear from them.

Typeset in Times New Roman 12/16 by
SJmagic DESIGN SERVICES, India.
Printed and bound in the UK by CPI Group (UK) Ltd.

Pen & Sword Books Limited incorporates the imprints of Atlas, Archaeology, Aviation, Discovery, Family History, Fiction, History, Maritime, Military, Military Classics, Politics, Select, Transport, True Crime, Air World, Frontline Publishing, Leo Cooper, Remember When, Seaforth Publishing, The Praetorian Press, Wharncliffe Local History, Wharncliffe Transport, Wharncliffe True Crime and White Owl.

For a complete list of Pen & Sword titles please contact
PEN & SWORD BOOKS LIMITED
George House, Units 12 & 13, Beevor Street, Off Pontefract Road,
Barnsley, South Yorkshire, S71 1HN, England
E-mail: enquiries@pen-and-sword.co.uk
Website: www.pen-and-sword.co.uk

Or
PEN AND SWORD BOOKS
1950 Lawrence Rd, Havertown, PA 19083, USA
E-mail: Uspen-and-sword@casematepublishers.com
Website: www.penandswordbooks.com

Contents

Acknowledgements   vii
Notes to Readers   x
Prologue   xiv

PART I – PRELUDE TO THE INVASION OF ENGLAND
Danish raid on Lindisfarne to William the Conqueror setting sail for England

PART II – THE LOST BATTLEFIELD
Landing, encampment, march to battle, battle and rout

Chapter 1	Battle of Hastings – the Greater Battlefield Topography	22
Chapter 2	The Saxon Port of Hastings and Norman Pre-Battle Camp	32
Chapter 3	Saxon and Norman Strategic Considerations	51
Chapter 4	Did the Normans Land at Pevensey or Hastings?	55
Chapter 5	How was the Fleet Disposed After Landing?	61
Chapter 6	Erecting the Upper and Lower Forts at Hastings	66
Chapter 7	King Harold Selects his Battlefield – the Highest Hill	74
Chapter 8	The Normans March to Battle	80
Chapter 9	The Battle	89
Chapter 10	Rout	118
Chapter 11	The Mount	125

Chapter 12	Burials	131
Chapter 13	The Battlefield that wasn't	134

APPENDICES

Appendix 1	The Sedlescombe Hoard	146
Appendix 2	Comparison of Battlefields, Traditional with Blackhorse Hill	149
Appendix 3	Consideration of the Traditional Battle Abbey Battlefield: the Route and March Time from Wilting Camp	152
Appendix 4	The Wastings	154
Appendix 5	Memorials	156
Appendix 6	Archaeology	159
Appendix 7	Senlac	162
Appendix 8	The Mount Revisited	163
Summary of Evidence		164

PART III – THE CONQUEST OF ENGLAND

March on Dover	176
Norman Army's March on London	177
The Coronation of Duke William	179
The Crushing of the English Rebellion and Devastation of the North	180
Domesday Survey	181
Death of William	182

Consequences	184
Bibliography/Sources	187
Notes	189
Index	199

Acknowledgements

First and foremost, the author owes a debt of gratitude to Nick Austin, author of the acclaimed *Secrets of the Norman Invasion*, for the extensive research and foundational work which resulted in a book with another battle site. Without it, this book would never have been written. In particular, I am grateful to him for his brilliance in locating and studying the site of the old Saxon burh at Wilting Farm, used by William the Conqueror as his advanced camp; for realising the significance of Redgeland Wood to the story and for identifying the general locality of the old Cinque Port of Hastings. These were all crucial to setting this book on the right road.

We must not forget the tireless, but unfortunately, unsuccessful effort that Nick Austin made trying to prevent the construction of the A2690 link road across Combe Haven water meadows. The haven, once an inland water connected to the sea, is an area of high natural beauty. The road, running from east to west, necessitating a deep cut at its eastern end resulted in the destruction of a large part of the old Saxon burh with Roman origins. But all is not lost, at least his findings (and photographs) are there for posterity and future researchers, including this one, to examine.

We should be grateful for the nineteenth-century builders of the Hastings to London railway line and its high supporting embankment for limiting the expansion of the modern town of Hastings westwards, thereby preserving the site of the old port of Hastings, the old Saxon burh at Wilting Farm, the Norman pre-battle camp area and Combe Haven itself.

We are most grateful to the Bayeux Tapestry Museum, Bayeux, Normandy, for making available the beautiful images of the Battle of Hastings from the tapestry to grace this book, without which a meaningful book would not have been possible.

The author wishes to thank Alex Vincent for his kind permission to use the excellent photographs of the Roman road (Kent Street) in his book *Roman Roads of Sussex*, one passing near to Sedlescombe and the other through it. King Harold's army must have used these roads in its march from London to form the shield wall defences at Blackhorse Hill.[1] Thanks are also due to Kent Archaeological Trust for permission to reproduce its sketch of a draught furnace, a type that might have been used to smelt iron ore in the Beauport bloomer.

Thanks are due to John Leftwich, who unstintingly worked to produce most of the diagrammatic illustrations and ground profiles in the book. Without these, a fully comprehensible story could not have been told. The illustrations depended upon the three-dimensional scale model of the greater battlefield that he painstakingly created, a model which additionally provides a dramatic bird's eye view of events in 1066; if it is true that a picture is worth a thousand words, then the model must surely be invaluable to the epic story of the Battle of Hastings. John also undertook the tedious task of proofreading the book, resulting in a tome fit to grace the shelves of any high street bookshop.

Thanks are due to John Tucker, for his magnificent ink and watercolour wash rendering of the old Saxon port of Hastings then on the banks of Combe Haven water.

Thanks are extended to Colin Simmons, managing partner of Crowhurst Park Holiday Village, for accompanying this writer around the park on Blackhorse Hill whilst relating interesting historical facts about the area.

Thanks must go to Roger Dempster who was a crucial driver in persuading, nay challenging, this author to undertake the huge task of turning this author's theories about the Battle of Hastings into the

ACKNOWLEDGEMENTS

reality of a book. He also proofread the book which has, hopefully, eliminated all errors. Thanks also to Kate Worell and Mike Morris for reading text and offering suggestions for improvements and to Gaynor Haliday for professional copyediting.

Thanks for the times my daughter, Erika, came to deliver me from the frustrations of the all-too-frequent IT problems with her expertise and finding the artist, Roger Coggins (see below), and liaising with him to produce a wonderful dust jacket for this book and to my wife, Francine, for her forbearance and sometimes encouragement and toleration of lost time, when perhaps we could have been doing more together.

The superb dust jacket battle scene illustration painted by Roger Coggins is augmented with Bayeux Tapestry images courtesy of the Bayeux Museum.

Last, but not least, thanks go to Dr Peter Gardner who patiently read through this tome pointing out the inevitable contradictions in a work of this sort and sometimes recommending better turns of phrase to improve clarity and understanding.

Notes to Readers

Location of the Battle of Hastings

It is well known that the Battle of Hastings did not take place at Hastings, although the old Port of Hastings on Combe Haven played a crucial part in the logistical effort of William the Conqueror. But the location of the old port, until the work of Nick Austin and this author, has not been known. The traditionally recognised site of the battle at Battle Abbey is generally referred to as 'the Battle Abbey battlefield, or Battle Abbey battle site' – this site is 9 or so miles from the present-day Hastings.

Finding a suitable name for our battlefield was not difficult, as the area where the fighting took place (the main battle of the shield wall and the subsequent struggle during the rout after King Harold's death) is marked on an extract from the Ordnance Survey (OS) map of East Sussex (see next page) as 'Blackhorse Hill'. We conclude this is the location where the Battle of Hastings really happened, not Battle Abbey.

Later in this book, we discuss the significance of Blackhorse Hill and other named features and the likelihood of their association with the 1066 battle. Suffice to say that black horses appear to play an important part in the psyche of Duke William, if not the Norman army as a whole; black horse images appear in number in the Bayeux Tapestry. There is also a popular story that William was gifted a huge black Andalusian warhorse by King Alfonso of Spain. Although no authentication can be found for it, the contemporary Chronicler,

NOTES TO READERS

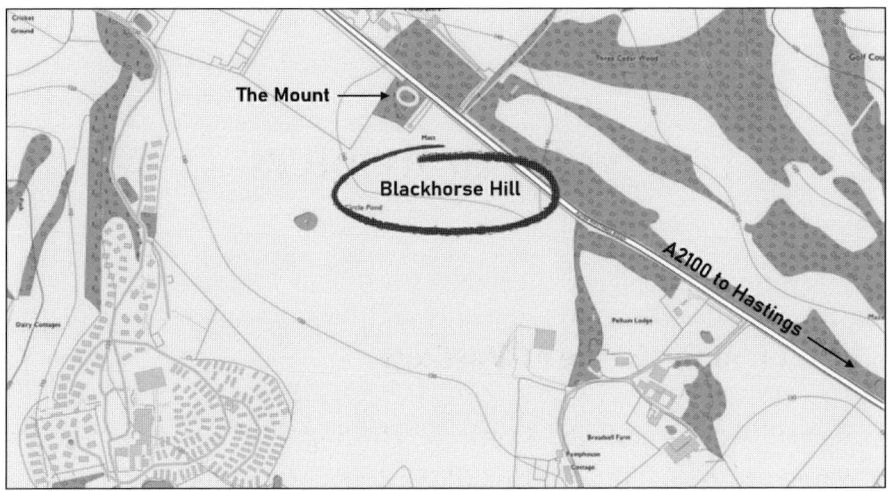

Ordnance Survey map showing 'Blackhorse Hill' (ringed) – Crown © Copyright 2021.

William of Poitiers, relates the competition between the brothers, Sancho and Alfonso, sons of King Ferdinand I of Castile, for the hand in marriage of a daughter of William the Conqueror. If Poitiers' account is correct, then there is some basis for the story of the gifting to William being true, adding weight to the meaning of black horses in our story.

Therefore, it seems reasonable to refer to the battle site as Blackhorse Hill, and that is the name adopted for the site of the battle throughout this book.

Systems of measurement

Here we explain the systems of measurement used in this book. By systems we mean metric and imperial measurement systems as well as the necessary use of antiquated measurement systems. Land elevation measurements are metric, in metres (m). This is because Ordnance Survey maps were converted from imperial to metric many decades ago and the 1:25,000 Explorer maps, with their 5m contour interval is convenient and well understood; as far as is known there were no land elevation measurements carried out in the medieval period.

Distance measurements are in imperial units, miles and feet (ft). This is because in the UK, miles are still very much in use and using feet is consistent with that, and importantly, this writer feels that metric measurements for distance are not in keeping with a book about a wholly historical subject. Land measurements are given in acres and hides; hides are of necessity retained as they appear in the ancient texts quoted and conversion where necessary to feet and square feet into acres seems reasonable.

Yards are retained when quoting from books written before the era of metrication in the UK.

Language

Throughout this book, English and Saxon are used and apart from their employment to describe a language, the words are interchangeable and are intended to mean the same thing, a people. Sometimes we use Anglo-Saxon instead of Saxon and this should be taken to mean the same.

Beauport

Beauport Park, the ancient wooded area partly on Blackhorse Hill, and part of the battlefield, is sometimes described in the book as Beauport Wood. The descriptions are interchangeable and mean the same place. The name was first used in the later eighteenth century. The woods, in Roman (and at later times) were a rich source of iron and the remains of a large Roman bloomery (described in the Chapter 1) and signs of occupation can still be seen today. It is thought that iron smelting pre-dating the Roman occupation may have taken place in the area.

NOTES TO READERS

Combe Haven

Combe Haven, identified on the 1:25,000 OS Explorer map as a stream draining into the English Channel through a tunnel under the Bulverhythe Road and under the east/west railway and through a 'cut' at Bulverhythe, has a major place in our story. Today, Combe Haven forms several square miles of inland wetlands that often floods in winter. At the time of the battle, Combe Haven was open to the sea at Bulverhythe, with Bulverhythe possibly forming an island. We have argued that the old Cinque Port of Hastings once stood on the eastern banks of Combe Haven.

Castel

Readers will notice that the word castle is sometimes spelt 'castel' in this book. This is the nineteenth-century spelling of the word in some books quoted. It has been decided to retain this archaic spelling where it occurs – it is not a spelling error.

Prologue

Much has been written and said about the Battle of Hastings, fought in 1066, the most memorable date in English history. The confrontation, tradition has it, took place on land neighbouring the town of Battle in Sussex. Battle and its abbey were founded by Norman monks to commemorate that epic confrontation and to remember and atone for the lives lost all those centuries ago. Readers studying the history may even have wondered why the battle came to take the name of Hastings, a town lying on the coast some 9 miles distant to the southeast of Battle. Questioning the name's origin is understandable, but as this book shows, Hastings is a fitting name for the battle. When the battle first came to be associated with Hastings is difficult to determine, but from accounts in *The Chronicle of Battel Abbey from 1066 to 1176* (henceforth referred to as *Chronicle of Battle Abbey*) we can deduce that it must have been when, or shortly after, the battle took place.

To unravel the true course of a history, historians must take care to avoid creating impressions based upon conjectures only, no matter how beautifully ranged these might be. Indulging in speculation serves only to confuse and mislead. This book aims to avoid speculation when dependence on presumptions would indeed lead readers to that outcome. Occasionally, when dealing with peripheral issues, and where concrete evidence is lacking but it benefits the continuity and flow of the story, the most likely course of events is given. Where such conjecture is used, that it is conjecture, will be clear.

PROLOGUE

The Battle of Hastings, along with the Roman conquest of Britain in the early centuries of the first Millennium, were major turning points in English and British history. It meant that a long-established Saxon kingdom was supplanted by Norman rule; the outcome of this battle was decided on just one day, 14 October 1066; a king died on the battlefield and a Norman duke was now destined to become king in his stead. Thereafter, Saxon lands were appropriated and parcelled out to barons and nobles, leading churchmen were replaced with Norman clerics and the land henceforth governed in the French language.

The English peoples were largely consigned to a life of subservience. But most of all, there was a cultural shift, everything changed and the country was, for the next three centuries, a two-language nation. The native language lost the greater part of the original Old English vocabulary and at the same time adopted nearly 10,000 French words, of which three-quarters still remain in use today.

This book has been divided into three parts. Part I covers the emergence of the Vikings on the Scandinavia West Coast, expansion westward across the North Sea and North Atlantic, and colonisation of what became Normandy in Northern France. It deals in some detail with the political situation leading up to the decision of Duke William of Normandy to invade England to take what he considered his rightful inheritance after King Edward the Confessor died in January 1066. Part II, the main part, sets out the ground-breaking findings; the evidence for the Battle of Hastings having been fought at Blackhorse Hill, some 2 miles east of the traditional site at Battle Abbey.

The book rounds off with Part III covering the Norman army's march on London following their great victory on 14 October 1066; the duke's coronation on Christmas Day and events leading up to King William I's death in 1087. Part II covers just over two weeks of our story, so that the preceding and following Parts provide a necessary context, an easy entry and exit so to speak, for what, at times, are analytical passages requiring the reader to give more attention to what they are reading – not always bedtime material.

The site at Battle, East Sussex, cannot be, and is not, ignored, as it is the traditionally accepted site with an almost folklore-ish resonance.

However, this book's main task is to carefully examine the considerable evidence for an alternative site, a site where this writer believes the battle actually took place. By comparing the topography of this battlefield and its surrounding area with contemporary accounts and other evidence, it is hoped to do justice to the claims made. Whether this objective has been sufficiently met, is for the reader to decide.

It is surprising that for such an important and well-known battle, the contemporary accounts, though providing much information, were so often patchy in detail, occasionally contradictory, and often difficult to interpret. The most singular omission in the ancient accounts is a clearly defined location for the battle, a location defined by its relationship to geographical features that can readily be identified today. However, enough topographical detail is provided in these accounts to enable beneficial comparison with modern cartographical sources, notably OS maps and Google Earth (GE) satellite imaging. The latter's powerful tools were unavailable to researchers until very recently and without them this book would not have been possible.

The book is designed to appeal to the general reader with an interest in history as well as the history professional who may wish to skip parts I and III.

PART I

PRELUDE TO THE INVASION OF ENGLAND

Danish raid on Lindisfarne to William the Conqueror setting sail for England

Saxons and Normans

Viking Raid on Lindisfarne

The holy brothers of the monastery at Lindisfarne, the island just off the Northumbrian coast known as Holy Island, we can suppose, were out tending their crops one fine June day, when suddenly something truly awesome was sighted: a squadron of square-rigged vessels, their sails ballooning, fast approaching their bit of coast. Living by the shore, the monks would have often seen ships passing, but nothing like this; they were larger and sleeker than anything they had seen before. We can expect that at first they were immobilised by the sight, but as the ships drew closer, they could see that the visitors were not friendly. The craft were packed with helmeted men brandishing, threateningly, axes, swords and spears glinting in the sun.

The monks being men of peace and unarmed were terrified, and would have dropped their implements and taken off across the sands in the hope of saving themselves. They had no chance; for the invaders were Vikings who had crossed the North Sea from Norway in their longboats in search of whatever they could seize.

Monks were struck down as they fled, their treasures plundered, church desecrated and their crops laid waste. Those not killed outright were dragged away in chains to be taken away to slavery, with others thrown over the side of the boats as the invaders set out back to whence they had come. The Vikings had no sooner debarked than they were gone. There is no detailed account of this episode, but the *Anglo-Saxon Chronicles* provides an outline of this catastrophe:

> In this year [AD 793] came dreadful forewarnings over the land of Northumbria, terrifying the people most woefully: there were immense sheets of lightning and whirlwinds, and fiery dragons were seen flying through the sky. A great famine soon followed these signs and not long after in the same year, on the sixth day before the ides [15] of January, the harrowing inroads of heathen men destroyed the church of God in Lindisfarne by robbery and slaughter.

Lindisfarne had been established by Aidan, an Irish Monk in the previous century, who had come to re-establish Christianity in the region.

Historians now consider that the January date for the raid is wrong and that a summer raid was more probable, when taking into account that longboats packed with fighting men could easily become swamped and capsize in the towering waves of the North Sea, so frequent in winter.

Our story of the Battle of Hastings and our quest for the site of the battlefield has its roots in the communities of Scandinavian people settled in the fjords of Norway and lower lying lands to the south on the Jutland peninsula and its associated islands. Those inhabiting the Norwegian fjords were known as Vikings or Norsemen and those on Jutland as Danes, giving rise to the political name, Denmark, for Jutland.

Emergence of the Vikings

Subsisting must have been precarious, especially in the fjords of the west coast of Norway, hemmed in by impassable mountains, the only outlet being to the sea – the North Sea. A diet of fish must have been the prime source of sustenance. Perhaps at first there were plentiful shoals of fish easily caught from their primitive craft fishing safely close inshore. As the population grew, more seaworthy boats designed and constructed for the more hazardous seas outside the fjord would have been needed.

One can suppose they ventured further and further out into the North Sea in search of ever better catches or even just out of curiosity and bravado. Once out in the stormy seas to the west, their vessels were tested to the utmost and no doubt there were many disasters before design improvements resulted in the longboat that has captured the imagination to this day. These longboats were open to the elements, were up to 60ft long, clinker built and could be sailed or rowed and no doubt were, in favourable conditions, very fast.

Discovery of the British Isles

As they sailed ever westwards, gaining in confidence and experience, they would eventually come across the east coast of the British Isles. They might have gone ashore and seen the developed agriculture and relative wealth of the Anglo-Saxon settlers and thought about how they might appropriate, or perhaps we should say misappropriate, some of this wealth.

The scene was set for raiding parties to seize some of these easy pickings and they returned home and armed themselves; so heralding the launch of 250 years of raids on the British Isles (including Ireland) leading to armies attacking the English realm and later settlement of large areas of northern England. The raid on Lindisfarne was followed by other raids mainly on remote religious communities, but by the end of the eighth century, the Norwegian Vikings had turned their attention to the Isles of Shetland and Orkney. Not a great deal is known of the events leading to the colonisation of these islands; although they may have at first come as raiders, perhaps there was little to raid, and instead they preoccupied themselves settling the many islands of these archipelagos where the population was too small to put up any serious resistance.

SAXONS AND NORMANS

Discovery and Settlement of Faroes, Iceland, Greenland and Vinland

Later, perhaps the Vikings from their bases in Orkney and Shetland ventured westward again discovering and settling Iceland in the 870s. The distances, in open boats, were considerable but not impossible, given their seaworthiness and sailing qualities, at least in summer. The Faroes are some 150 miles from Shetland and Orkney, and Iceland a further 250 miles. It was not a journey to be made in winter. Greenland, with its eastern ice sheet a mile in height, can on rare occasions in clear air and in ideal light conditions, be seen from Iceland. Those early settlers in Iceland would have been tempted to cross over to explore what are now known as the Denmark Straits, to take a look. In fact, Icelandic settlers and Norwegians under the leadership of Erik the Red did just that. From the late tenth century until the fifteenth century, Greenland hosted a viable community until the climate turned against them; the remains of their habitations are still visible today.

Later, the North American continent was visited, possibly discovered by vessels being blown off course, missing Greenland and landing up on the northern tip of Newfoundland where signs of a Norse settlement were found in 1960 at a place named L'anse aux Meadows (in English, Cove of Meadows) which needs no further explanation. There are several interpretations of the French name; the most likely is that it derived its name from a French navigational chart.

Danish Vikings Raid England

It was the Danes who next took an interest in the Anglo-Saxon kingdoms, raiding far and wide, as well as northern Europe. Sources are scarce and confusing but point to a Ragnar Lodrok as the leader of these raids. In 835, Sheppey in the Thames estuary was attacked.

This was followed by raids on Southampton (840), Portland (840) and London and Rochester (842). These forays gradually changed in nature as the forces increased in size and were better equipped to the extent they could avoid the dangerous journey home to Scandinavia and remain in England throughout the winter. By the 850s, Danes wintered over on the Isle of Thanet (now joined to Kent, but still retaining its Isle prefix).

Danish Occupation and Settlement of Northern England

This was the beginning of something much more dangerous for Saxon England. The numbers of invaders were far greater, they were learning to subsist from the land on a permanent basis and they were clearly harbouring ambitions to occupy England. This indicates that their army was numerous, experienced and well equipped or the Saxons just too weak to defend their lands, or both. In 865, the sons of Ragnar Lodbrok, particularly Halfdene or Halfdan Ragnarsson, leading 'The Great Heathen Army', conquered Mercia and Northumbria, taking York (Jorvik) in 866 or 867 (according to whichever source is used). Lands taken from Anglo-Saxons were parcelled out and some amongst them stayed to farm them, showing they were intending to remain. In 869, in the next stage of the Danish invasion, they seized East Anglia, killing its king, Edmund, in a most grisly manner.

King Edmund of East Anglia, leading his army in defence of his kingdom was defeated and captured. When he refused to rule as an under-lord owing allegiance to Halfdene, he was tied to a tree, and killed by a volley of arrows, it was said, until he took on the appearance of a porcupine, and was then beheaded. The king became a martyr and was honoured as a saint, giving rise to the town's present-day name of Bury St Edmunds and a place of pilgrimage throughout the Middle Ages. Although this is but an aside to this prelude, to this writer it has been a symbol of the ruthlessness and cruelty of the Vikings of the period.

SAXONS AND NORMANS

Danes Attack Wessex

The invading army, not allocated Anglo-Saxon lands conquered in the north, regrouped and in 871 turned their attention to Wessex, the last kingdom in England still free of Danes. They marched up the Thames valley to Reading where they were met by the Wessex army under King Ethelred and his younger brother Alfred. The Danes successfully fended off the Saxon army, but shortly afterwards the Danes, under Halfdene, were defeated at the Battle of Ashdown, somewhere near to the Uffington White Horse and the ancient pre-Roman Uffington Castle in Berkshire.

That year Ethelred died, it is thought from battle wounds received at Ashdown, and was succeeded by Alfred. Thus began a long, for the time, twenty-eight-year reign that was largely spent resisting the Danish army from conquering and occupying Wessex and turning England into a Danish kingdom. A great era in English history had begun with the heroic efforts of King Alfred being remembered to this day and immortalised with statues of Alfred the Great, the only English king honoured with the title 'Great' at Winchester, Wantage (Alfred's birth place) and Pewsey.

Alfred the Great Defends Wessex

Alfred's reign, though, did not start off well. The Danes, after Ashdown, withdrew back to London then to Mercia, after being paid to go away and pillage somewhere else. But they returned in strength later in the decade (870s) and attacked by land and sea. There followed a disaster for the Danes. Sailing along the south coast of England in search of a landing place some of their fleet were wrecked on the Isle of Purbeck (not actually an island) demonstrating the vulnerability of the type of craft that they, and later William the Conqueror, used in invasions of England. This, as we shall see in part II of this book, adds weight to the argument that Duke William did not land his boats on the exposed beaches of West Sussex, but in the sheltered inlet of Combe Haven.

The Danes briefly occupied Wareham and Exeter then left under a truce with hostages exchanged, but it was not long before they were back in early 878. The attack, now under a leader called Guthrum, overwhelmed the Wessex army and Alfred was driven into hiding. Thus began the period which includes the incident of popular mythology of Alfred receiving a scolding from the lady of the house in which he was hiding incognito from the Danes and then burning the cakes he was supposed to be attending. True or false, this was Alfred's low point when Wessex was close to becoming a Danish kingdom and all of England ruled by a Danish king. Alfred had fled to the Isle of Athelney in what are now known as the Somerset levels in the south-western part of Somerset. The levels are low lying at or about 10ft (3m) above mean sea level and although drained in the seventeenth century by the Dutch, are still liable to flooding today. At the time of Alfred, the levels largely consisted of tall reed beds and water channels difficult to navigate except by local people who lived there and knew their way around.

Alfred Defeats Danes and Treaty of Wedmore

From this base, Alfred, with a small band of followers, harried the Danes until eventually he was able to marshal an army which took on the Danes at Ethandune (also known as Edington) on the Wiltshire Downs and, after a great victory and a siege at Chippenham, the Danes capitulated. In the treaty that followed, the Treaty of Wedmore, Guthrum was obliged to convert to Christianity and remove his army from Wessex. This created what later came to be known as Danelaw, the area of England north-east of the line between London and Chester, essentially along the line of Watling Street, where the Danes ruled. Guthrum adopted the Saxon name Athelstan.

Alfred, a devout Christian who in his youth had visited Rome, adopted a policy of reconciliation with Guthrum, entertaining him and giving him presents. Whether this was an entirely philanthropic

Christian gesture or expediency, or both, we'll never know. But the result was that Guthrum and his Danish army left Wessex in peace, returning to East Anglia and settling the lands. Guthrum may have turned out to be an asset to Alfred, deterring later Danish invaders who, also faced with the returning strength of Wessex, increasingly found it more profitable to raid Northern France. This historical event was the genesis of the dukedom of Normandy and the Normans. It could be argued that the battle of Ethandune, though not an event that stands out in popular history, was a major turning point and without that English victory, the Danes would have had enough territory to settle and administer and the French kings (Capet dynasty) could easily have dealt with the Danes who came in smaller numbers in search of booty.

However, King Alfred was still faced by raiding expeditions, although the Wessex army, and recently established navy, was up to the task of preserving the integrity of the kingdom of Wessex. The greatest threat to Alfred came from Haesten, the commander of a new Danish army, arriving after an unsuccessful raid on Northern France to attack Kent. It seems the defenders in France were too strong and Haesten thought Kent too far from Wessex for Alfred to do anything about it, but he was wrong. Alfred negotiated with Haesten, which resulted in his sons being baptised into the Christian faith and the Danish commander taking his men to Essex, from where they organised unsuccessful attacks on Exeter, London and Farnham where Alfred's son, Edward, won a victory over the Danes. By 896, the latest Danish army had split, some settling on land already in Danish hands, others returning to France to renew their attempts to conquer and occupy lands there.

Alfred against the odds had secured Wessex, but with the Danes in possession of half of England. In the remaining years of Alfred's life, he initiated the construction of fortified towns, or burhs, stretching from Exeter in the west to Hastings in the east and as far north as Worcester. But Alfred was not only a warrior king – it was he who had established the Royal Navy – he was literate and well read. He was a lawmaker, an educator, and one who strengthened the religious establishment that had begun to falter even before the pressure from Norwegian and Danish invaders who hated the Christian religion. Alfred took the existing laws of the kingdoms of England and codified them into the *Doom Book (domboc)*. He had religious works translated into English, and even included one on general history that his subjects could read and thereby be better educated.

Alfred died at Winchester in 899 and was buried in the town's minster. Alfred's latter years were more peaceful than for most of his reign, but Danish incursions were still a nuisance to him especially their attacks on London, which he had incorporated into the kingdom of Wessex. But Alfred had successfully preserved Wessex as an Anglo-Saxon realm for which he was deservedly honoured and remembered as Alfred the Great. He was succeeded by his son Edward (the Elder).

King Athelstan

Edward the Elder, confusingly known as King Edward I (there being a new line of Edwards following the Norman Conquest), reigned almost as long (twenty-six years) as his father. He consolidated his rule on southern England and extended his domain into Mercia. He defeated an army invading from Northumbria and conquered remaining areas occupied by Danes in southern England. By this point in the book, readers may have concluded that medieval kings spent most of their time defending their realms against outside forces, or attacking neighbouring lands or suppressing rebellious forces and they would be right. Edward's son, Athelstan, faced just that when Edward died in 925 and rebel forces plotted, unsuccessfully, to deprive him of the succession.

King Athelstan is probably one of the most unsung hero kings in English history by the general public today, being overshadowed by the deeds of his grandfather, King Alfred. Although his reign was relatively short in comparison to his predecessors, at only fourteen years, his achievements in conquering new lands in England were quite outstanding. He can truly be called the first king of the English and the first overlord ruling over England.

When the Viking king, Sihtric of York, died, Athelstan seized the chance to invade York. His growing power base was such that he was able to gain dominion over North Wales, and in 927 the Scottish king recognised Athelstan as his overlord, establishing the borders of England with both Wales and Scotland. Later, Cornwall came under his sway and he even created a bishopric there. Like his grandfather, Athelstan reformed the legal system and supported religious communities.

King Constantine, the Scottish king, looked to shake off Athelstan's lordship but, at the Battle of Brunanburh in 937, was decisively defeated by Athelstan, securing his domain for the Saxons for the next seventy-seven years. He died on 2 October 939, William of Malmesbury telling us:

> King Athelstan died at Gloucester. His noble remains were conveyed to Malmesbury [Wiltshire] and buried under the altar. Many gifts, both in gold and silver, as well as relics of saints purchased abroad in Brittany, were carried before the body … and there … amassed, and left untouched. His years, though few, were full of glory.

King Athelstan granted about 600 acres (243 hectares) of land to the men of Malmesbury for their assistance in fighting the Danes, though the fighting was more about conquering lands than defending Wessex or England. The land known as Kings Heath is situated just outside Malmesbury and is to this day held by the burgesses and freemen of Malmesbury.

Now we look to the Vikings' switch to invading Northern France.

Viking Invasion of France

The Treaty of Wedmore made it difficult for new waves of Danes crossing the North Sea to gain a foothold on English soil. Firstly, the kingdom of Wessex was by then too strong to be dislodged and secondly, those Danes already settled seem to have resented any newcomers or rejected them because of their agreement with the kings of Wessex. There may have been some exceptions where new Danish settlers were accepted, particularly in Northumbria.

We have already seen the Vikings raiding France during the latter part of the ninth century, using the rivers as a conduit and even reaching Paris. But it seems by the tenth century they were increasingly managing to settle areas of northern France. In 911, Rollo, leader of an incursion of, it is thought, Danes and Norwegians (Norsemen) deep into France, was defeated at Chartres. This defeat resulted in the French king, Charles III, acknowledging, in the Treaty of St Claire sur Epte, Rollo as occupant of the lands between the Seine and Rouen which he had already conquered in exchange for his allegiance and help in defending against further Viking raids. He was baptised a year later.

The Dukes of Normandy

Not a great deal is known of this period, but Rollo became the Count of Rouen, either self-proclaimed or granted. During the reign of Richard II, Rollo's great grandson, the title count gave way to duke, no doubt in recognition of the extension of their rule westwards, and the lands became known as the Duchy of Normandy, and the Viking settlers, Normans from the general name, Norsemen.

Normans, like their forefathers, were noted warriors and from Normandy launched an invasion and colonisation of Sicily. The Normans were quick to adopt the institutions they encountered in France. Foremost was their taking up the French language – in the form of Norman French – and Christianity, founding Norman monasteries as centres of learning. They built great motte and bailey castles, which became the centrepiece of Norman rule after the Norman Conquest in England, and they took to the horse, which they brought to England in 1066 and used in numbers at the Battle of Hastings.

The 3rd Duke, Robert the Devil, inherited the duchy in 1027. He was the father of Duke William, William the Conqueror, by a tanner's daughter named Herleva. They were not married so Robert's son became known as William the Bastard, a title he may have worn with pride, in line with his reputation as a cruel and uncompromising warrior.

King Cnut (or Canute)

Seven Saxon kings ruled England following the death of King Athelstan, Edmund Ironside's reign being the last before the Danes invaded the kingdom in force again, ruling for more than two decades. Although Danish incursions had restarted in the 980s and 990s with King Ethelred (the Unready) paying Danegeld to the Danish king after the Battle of Maldon in 991, it had been a period of relative peace and stability.

But things were about to change. In 1013, the Danish king, Sweyn Forkbeard, invaded England, perhaps as a result of the St Brice's Day massacre of Danes who had settled in England. Ethelred was forced to flee to Normandy and Sweyn took the throne but died a year later and Ethelred re-occupied it. But after a long reign of thirty-seven years he died, being succeeded by his son Edmund (Ironside) in April 1016. Edmund's reign was short and bloody, fighting against the invasion of Danish forces led by Cnut. At the Battle of Assandun, on 18 October 1016, Edmund was defeated and the two protagonists agreed to split the kingdom, but following the death of Edmund on 30 November (perhaps dying from battle wounds), Cnut took the English throne exiling Edmund's sons, Edward (in time to become King Edward the

Confessor) and Arthur, to Normandy. Later, Cnut became king of Denmark and king of Norway and was known as Cnut the Great.

Cnut reigned from 1016 until 1035 and although he was ruthless, often necessary in those times to deal with threats to rule and to stabilise the realm, he was generally regarded as a wise and effective king. He had been baptised into Christianity before taking the throne, he supported the church and integrated Danelaw into English law.

He is popularly known for the episode – described (or invented) by Henry of Huntingdon a century later – to hold back the tide. In an act of humility to show that the power of kings was worthless set against the divine, he set his throne on the shoreline and commanded the tide not to rise. When the tide inevitably rose and his legs were in the sea, he is said to have taken off his crown and never worn it again.

Cnut, along with St Edmund, Alfred, Athelstan, Edmund Ironside, Edward the Confessor and Harold II, is another of those landmark kings who shaped English history. He died on 12 November 1035 at Shaftesbury and his bones kept in boxes along with other early Saxon rulers (the boxes are on view in Winchester Cathedral). His son Harold ruled England for five years having usurped the throne from Harthacnut, his half-brother, who was older and next in line to the throne. Harthacnut was away in Denmark ruling as king of Denmark when his father died and was unable to press his claim.

When Harold I himself died, in 1040, Harthacnut ascended the throne but reigned for just two years, and it is said, died from excess of drink at a wedding ceremony.

King Edward the Confessor and the Godwins

Edward, son of Ethelred the Unready, had returned from exile to England in 1041 at the invitation of Harthacnut, possibly because Harthacnut knew he was dying, and wanted to recognise him as his heir. When Harthacnut died, Edward inherited the realm and was crowned king of England at Winchester on 3 April 1043.

His rule was turbulent, and lacking a strong power base he was at odds for much of his reign with the Godwins who held earldoms and lands and had a following over large swathes of southern England. Thus was laid the road for the showdown in 1066 with Duke William of Normandy. Edward spent his early years in exile, mostly in Normandy. He was the son of Emma, a noblewoman (daughter of Richard I, Duke of Normandy), and would have been steeped in Norman ways favouring Normans over the Anglo-Saxon aristocracy. For instance, Edward brought Robert of Jumièges to England in 1042 (just prior to becoming king of England) making him Bishop of London, and subsequently, in 1051, Archbishop of Canterbury. Perhaps a lack of knowledge of English was a factor in these appointments, but he had no problem appointing Normans ahead of indigenous Anglo-Saxons. This led to much resentment among the English, who were often excluded from spiritual and secular positions.

Things came to a head in 1051, when relatives of Edward in northern France came to visit him – resulting in a brawl in Dover. When Godwin refused to obey Edward and punish the town's burgesses, Earl Godwin and his sons were forced into exile in Flanders and Edward sent his wife Edith, daughter of Godwin, to a nunnery.

But the Godwins' exile was untenable and they returned to England the following year, 1052. The circumstances of their return are not clear from the sources; some say it took an invasion of an army that the Godwins had collected together in exile, and others that his English power base was just too strong for the king to ignore. The Godwins' earldoms were restored and King Edward's wife was released from the nunnery and occupied her place as Queen of England again.

In 1053, Godwin died and his son Harold became Earl of Wessex; later Harold's brothers Gyrth, Leofwine and Tostig gained East Anglia, Middlesex and Northumbria respectively. The Godwins were arguably the most powerful clan in the land and in a position for one of the brothers to succeed Edward, with Harold, the eldest, being the main contender.

1066: THE LOST HASTINGS BATTLEFIELD

Duke William

Duke William inherited the title from his father Robert and became the 4th Duke of Normandy. He was born about 1028 in Falaise. Following Robert's death returning from a trip to Jerusalem, his illegitimate son, William, became duke of the Duchy of Normandy in 1035 at the tender age of 7. Remarkable as this may seem, Robert's nobles had pledged to him that on his death William would inherit the duchy. One can only understand how it was the pledge held, by assuming the alternative was war between the nobles and break-up of the duchy – all to the advantage of the king of France.

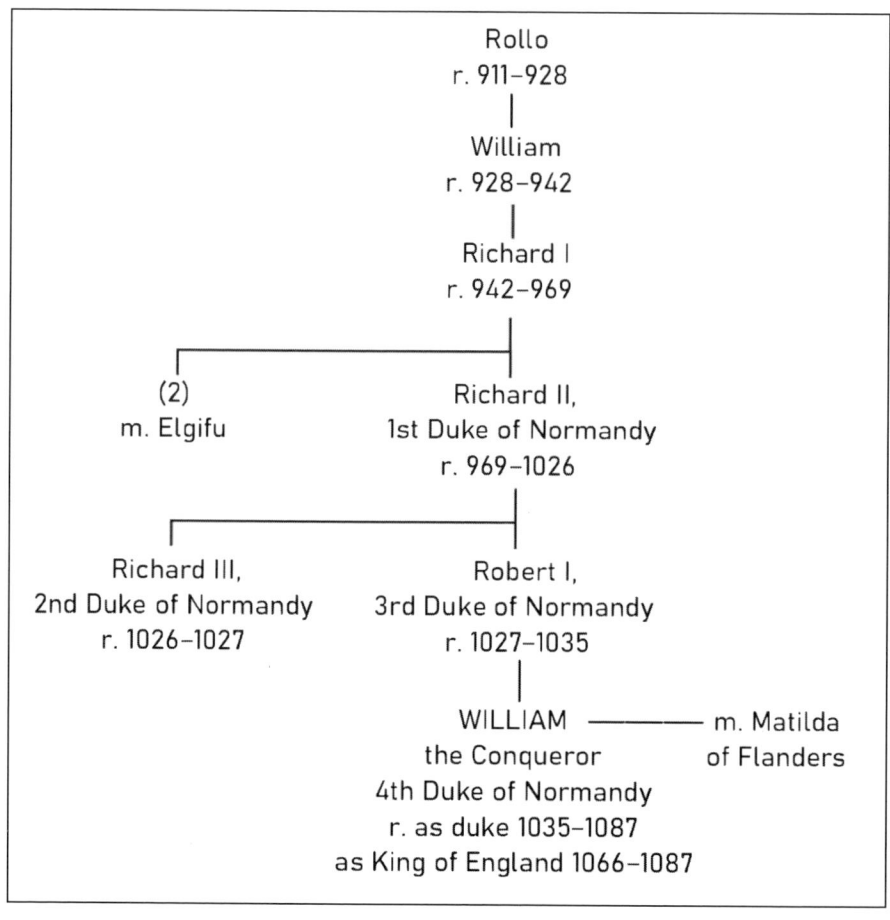

William was insulated at first from challenges to his title, being protected by his great-uncle the Archbishop of Rouen and later by King Henry I of France. But in 1047, when William had reached the age of about 20, he had to fight for the duchy and at the Battle of Val-es-Dunes in 1047 he met and defeated an army led by his cousin, Guy of Burgundy.

The next few years saw William consolidating his power base, establishing the boundaries of Normandy and defeating King Henry I (who turned against him) at the Battle of Mortimer in 1057. By 1060, Normandy was firmly under his rule and he was thoroughly schooled in the art of warfare. He eyed up the kingdom across the Channel and was ready to take it on militarily if necessary.

The Oath

We have seen that Edward the Confessor had been forced into exile at an early age and spent twenty-eight years of his life mostly in the Duchy of Normandy. This writer can find no evidence of Edward ever meeting Duke William. But it is inconceivable that he did not, given that the two were both living, at least some of the time, coincidentally in Normandy for a period of thirteen years, with one being the son of a king and the other the son of a duke and a duke himself for six of those years. If there was an affinity between them despite their age differences then that would have consequences.

So it was; according to chronicler William of Jumièges, Edward sent his archbishop to Rome visiting Duke William on the way to install the duke as heir to the English throne:

> Edward, king of the English having found himself without an heir had already sent [1051] Duke Guillaume Robert, Archbishop of Canterbury [also known as Robert de Jumièges] to the duke, installing the duke as heir to the kingdom that God had given him.

This account is quite plausible, given as we have seen King Edward's years in Normandy. But whether it was right for him to make a promise of the kingdom to a foreign duke, or anyone else, is another matter.

The chronicle continues, describing Earl Harold's crossing the Channel to visit Duke William:

> Later on he also sent Harold, the most important of all the counts [earls] of his kingdom by wealth, dignity and power, to the duke, guaranteeing the crown and to confirm the promise that was made according to Christian rites.

Harold made his preparations for crossing the sea and landed (in some accounts he was shipwrecked) in Pontieu, where he fell into the hands of Gui, Count of Abbeville, as well as his men, and was locked up under guard.

The duke (Duke William), as soon as he was informed of the fact, sent his men, who took Harold by force then forced him to stay with him for some time and made him accompany him on his incursion against the Bretons where Harold was to bravely rescue one of the Norman knights who had fallen into a swamp.

After Harold confirmed his loyalty to the kingdom of England, the duke promised him his daughter, Adelise, and half of the kingdom (no doubt as an underlord).

This story is much more controversial, even though the Bayeux Tapestry supports it – having scenes of Harold at Bosham in Hampshire prior to crossing to France. The tapestry is a memorial to the Norman Conquest of England commissioned, it has been thought, by Bishop Odo, William's half-brother. The tapestry was subsequently hung in Bayeux Cathedral as a propaganda piece, among other things, justifying William's claim to the throne and his invasion of England.

It is implausible, given Harold's power and status in England and an obvious contender for the throne, that he would have taken instruction from King Edward to go to Duke William to renew the pledge of the crown on his death, which he had made earlier in his reign. Another, and more likely version (to this writer), is that Harold set out across the Channel to obtain the release and return of his brother, Wulfnorth, and his nephew Hakon, both of whom had been made hostages in a hostage exchange made by King Edward.

These events occurred, it has been calculated, in 1064. It is reported in some accounts that William extracted Harold's support in succeeding to the crown of England when Edward the Confessor died. There is probably some truth in all this, but it is unlikely that Harold had any intention of giving up a strong claim to the throne when any promise he may have made had been under duress.

From Duke William's point of view this did not matter. All that mattered was that a promise had been made and he had a pretext to invade England and take the throne. William did not have long to wait.

Crowning of Harold; William Prepares to Invade England

At the end of 1065, King Edward fell ill; he died on 5 January 1066 and was buried in the Abbey at Westminster (actually the West Minster at the time consecrated just days beforehand). Harold Godwinson was crowned Harold II, king of England, the day after the funeral. Readers might think this was a bit hasty. Not surprising though, considering there were other claimants to the throne, including Duke William, the Norwegian king and others.

It would not have taken long for William's contacts in England to cross the Channel and report the event to him. Some accounts say William was furious – as one would expect. Perhaps though, he was secretly delighted, because here was the pretext for the invasion of England he needed – he must have known he would have to fight for the crown of England. He immediately began the assembly of a fleet of longboats, and the expansion of his Norman army, recruiting forces from his allies: Bretons, Flemish and even French. William at this time had sway over neighbouring lands and no doubt there would have been eager recruits expecting booty at the lower levels, and lands and appointments at the upper. The main construction site was on the River Dives between Cherbourg and the River Seine on the Normandy coast. The Dives offered a long, sheltered waterway where a fleet could be laid down and constructed with easy access to timber from the local hinterland.

Orderic Vitalis, son of a French priest, born in Shropshire, wrote in the early twelfth century that 'the Norman fleet, which for a month past had lain in the estuary of the Dive and harbours round about waiting for a south-west wind, was blown by a westerly wind into the region of St Valery.'

This account makes it sound like an involuntary move eastwards along the coast to St Valery. Whether or not this was so, St Valery on the Somme River, is a far more suitable jumping off place for the invasion fleet with a channel crossing half the distance to its destination in East Sussex. This was important because, as we shall see, the voyage could be made overnight from there and more secretly. In addition, the Normans would be exposed to the weather for less time, reducing the chances of swampings, wreckings and scattering of the fleet.

It seems the fleet had to wait in harbour at St Valery for the weather again and no doubt to pick up extra troops and, perhaps, horses.

The fleet set sail for England on the evening of Friday, 29 September 1066 after a long frustrating wait for a fair wind.

PART II

THE LOST BATTLEFIELD

Landing, encampment, march to battle, battle and rout

Chapter 1

Battle of Hastings – the Greater Battlefield Topography

In later chapters we will examine the approach to the Battle of Hastings at Blackhorse Hill, by both the Saxon and Norman armies, the battle itself, and the aftermath when the Saxon defence collapsed, ending in a headlong rout. In order to work out what happened and the location of these events, particularly the day-long struggle between the 'Saxon Wall' defence line and the mobile forces of Duke William, it is important to have an understanding of the topography of the battlefield itself, the greater battle area and Norman shore camp established after their landing at Combe Haven. Combe Haven was then a major sheltered inland tidal waterway with access to the English Channel.

Initial attempts to work out events and movements from the 1:25,000 OS map proved difficult, owing to the complex geography, especially the close-packed and winding contour lines often obscured by roads, buildings and other modern features. The solution was to construct an accurate three-dimensional scale model (Figures 1.1 and 1.2) for the whole area of interest, enabling comparison between contemporary descriptive records of the battle and the topography. The results were quite astounding, bringing the whole area to life. It became clear what could not have happened and what was possible on the pivotal day of 14 October 1066. A major benefit of this approach was that it made it possible to reproduce the topography to reflect the situation as it was thought to be at the time of the battle. In particular, the model shows

BATTLE OF HASTINGS

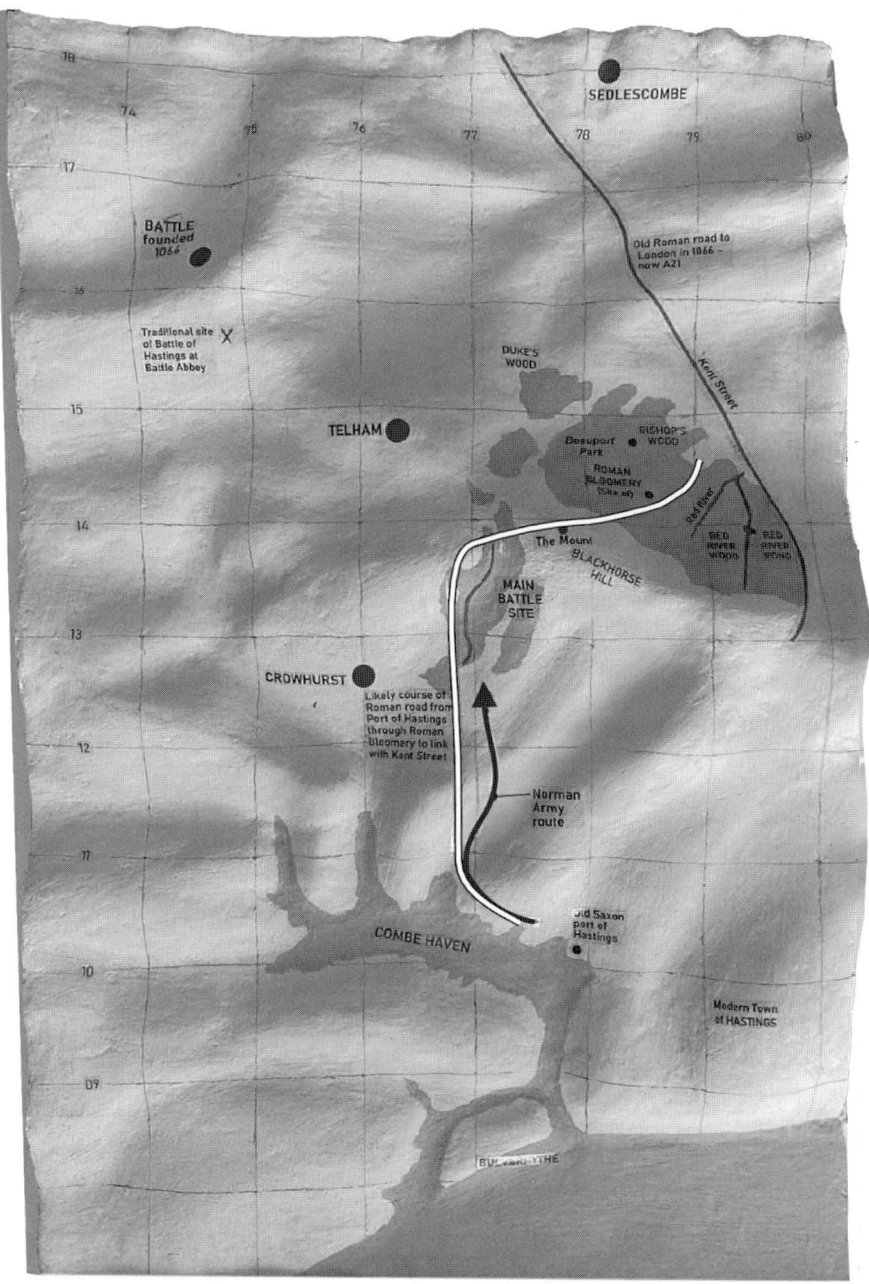

Figure 1.1 Three-dimensional model of the greater battle of Hastings area – image taken vertically. Note: each grid square is 1km, or 0.62 miles.

the entrance to Combe Haven lying west of Bulverhythe Island before becoming blocked when a series of late thirteenth-century storms heaped up masses of shingle. Subsequently, the haven itself became silted up due to lack of scouring flow.

The haven today is a wildlife nature reserve liable to flooding and is at, or just below, sea level. It retains its pre-land locked name, although not everywhere is recognisable as such, due to considerable land infill and buildings – work which continues to this day.

Readers will derive maximum benefit from the model if they have a basic understanding of medieval battlefield strategy. Army

Figure 1.2 Topographical model of the greater battle of Hastings area. Note: each grid square is 1km, or 0.62 miles. See colour plate section.

commanders would be watchful for flanking movements by their adversary, the success of which could lead to a break up of a formation as men and horses infiltrated behind their massed ranks. In the case of armies adopting a close defensive formation, as King Harold did, and if there were insufficient men to form a complete 360-degree protection (when that was the preferred option), then anchoring the flanks against an impenetrable feature, such as a cliff face, river, or dense woods,[1] would serve.

Medieval defending generals would also seek to occupy elevated ground with steep slopes making it virtually impossible to get at the defensive shield wall. Rising ground behind an army's defensive line, extending as far back as possible, would be sought as an insurance against the battle going badly and being forced into a fighting withdrawal. The worst situation for an army to find itself in was to be forced from the top of its hill with the enemy and its cavalry now bearing down with gravity on its side. This is best understood by referring to Figure App.2, Appendix 2 where we can see Harold's initial defensive position well down the slope on the steepest part.

If all was lost, a defeated army could save itself if it had terrain that provided quick escape routes and hopefully forest and woodland to melt away into. An attacking general would seek a safe and easy route to the battlefield or battle line; safe, so that the terrain passed through could not conceal troops waiting in ambush. The route to the battlefield would ideally be short and provide good going underfoot. This would ensure men, horses and, importantly, the baggage support train arrived fighting fit to face the enemy.

The defensive position on Blackhorse Hill occupied by King Harold meets all of these criteria.

Obviously, things are more complex than this, but commanders, as with the experienced King Harold and Duke William, would be on the look-out for any features and ground that could be used to advantage as the fight progressed. The model images are intended to assist readers relate the landscape to the chronicled battle descriptions, and to illustrate what events happened and where.

Location of The Old Port of Hastings

'Nobody knows where the old Hastings stood', wrote Petre Mais,[2] but thanks to Nick Austin's painstaking work, that is no longer the case. It was he who showed that the location of the concentration of William's forces before battle on Pevensey was wrong and made the case for the Norman lower base camp being at the eastern end of Combe Haven, along with the old Saxon port of Hastings. Austin arrived at this result based, it seems, on resistivity[3] mapping, lidar[4] imaging and visual examination of the ground surface itself.

Austin is precise about the location of Hastings[5] in his book, placing it at the north-western corner of the large inlet abutting Monkham Wood,[6] whereas on the marked-up lidar image, it is placed at the north-eastern corner, some 600ft (180m) apart, close to where this book places it.

Austin's work has been instrumental in helping this writer discover the visual remains of old Hastings on the GE imaging application; without this lead, this writer acknowledges, it would not have been possible to attempt this book. The curved red line marked on the GE image (Figure 2.8) distinguishes between land that was once tidal waters, deep enough for shipping (now wet lands liable to flooding), and land 1m above mean sea level. North of the line, we believe, lie the buried remains of the old port of Hastings, which satellite outlines appear to show in the enlarged image in Figure 2.10.

This inland waterway in 1066 provided Duke William with a safe anchorage and easy beaching for his 700 or so longboats; now we need to look at this important natural harbour in a bit more detail, it being a principal part of the Battle of Hastings scene. The 11½ miles of Combe Haven shoreline (measured at the 5m contour line) could easily accommodate William's fleet, even allowing for some of the haven's banks being unusable or too distant from the Norman encampment. We could expect that some of the boats would be drawn up out of the water after unloading. In fact, as we shall see, some boats were employed in the defensive perimeter at the lower fort.

But some authors have the Norman fleet drawn up on exposed beaches next to the sea. Julius Caesar, as we shall see later, familiar with the calmer waters of the Mediterranean tried that when he invaded Britain in 55 BC. But William's landing was not on the coast, the Norman longships sailed into Combe Haven as they would surely have planned to do before leaving Normandy – the suggestion of advanced planning here is touched on in Chapter 6.

Apart from Combe Haven, occupying a little under 10 per cent of the model area, the key points featuring large in this story, some of which are marked on the model, are:

- The old Roman road (Kent Street) by which we believe Harold's army approached the battlefield and those who survived escaped back to London.
- The Norman camp area stretching from the old Port of Hastings, beyond Redgeland Wood to Upper Wilting Farm, site of the ancient Anglo-Saxon burh. The area is a narrow strip of land, hemmed in and naturally protected by the haven to the south-east, the ridge, represented by Redgeland Wood to the north-east, and a chasm to the north-west. The whole expanse, just ¾ mile in length, by an average of ¼ mile wide (some 120 acres),[7] might be expected to accommodate an estimated 7,000 troops and 1,000 horses; an area quite cramped but not too large to fortify with ditches and embankments. Points to note:
- Blackhorse Hill battlefield and the Saxon Shield Wall lie on a spur branching southward from the Telham escarpment.
- The Red River in Beauport Wood into which Normans and Saxons may have tumbled during the rout phase of the battle.
- The route the Norman army would probably have taken to the battlefield from their camp at Old Hastings Port area.
- Other features, including: Bishop's Wood, Duke's Wood and Blackhorse Hill.

Of course, this book is about the site of the battle being at Blackhorse Hill, but the traditional site cannot be disregarded. Therefore, the model provides a useful way to demonstrate the relative positions of the two sites and the route the Norman army would have had to take from their base camp in the port of Hastings area to the Battle Abbey site, if the battle did indeed take place there. It is difficult to speculate upon the route the Norman army might have taken because it seems so improbable to this writer that the battle took place at the Battle Abbey site – this matter is dealt with in Appendix 3 to this book.

The battlefield area, some 2 miles to the north of the Norman camp, forms a ridge of complex elevated land running north-west to south-east to the sea at the post Conquest town of Hastings. The model (Figures 1.1 and 1.2) shows this ridge gradually rising from the east to its highest point on the present A2100 road. This road runs from the town of Battle south-eastwards to the northern edge of Hastings. Just north-eastward of the A2100 the land falls away to the River Brede valley lowlands.

The ridge forms the High Weald at the north-western end around the town of Battle where the elevation is about 70m rising to 141m at the highest point of Blackhorse Hill (location of the Saxon shield wall on 14 October 1066 – see Chapter 9) 2 miles to the south-east.

The land of the Norman camp, aforementioned, rises as part of the slope from present-day Hastings (on the western extremity adjacent to Combe Haven waters).

Roman Bloomeries and Roman Roads in East Sussex[8]

Iron production has been going on in Britain since ancient times and in particular in the Weald of Kent and Sussex, the latter being our area of interest. Production pre-dated the Roman invasion of AD 43 and Britain was one of their most important iron-producing provinces for the Romans. The bloomery at the forested area now known as Beauport Park[9] in East Sussex was the third most important in the Empire.

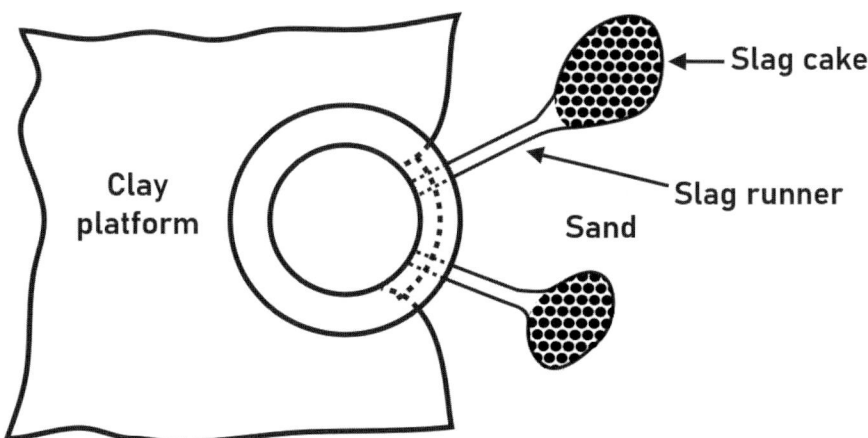

Figure 1.3 Sketch of natural-draught furnace at Ashwicken, Norfolk, one similar to that found at Holdbean Wood in Sussex. Courtesy Kent Archaeological Rescue Unit.

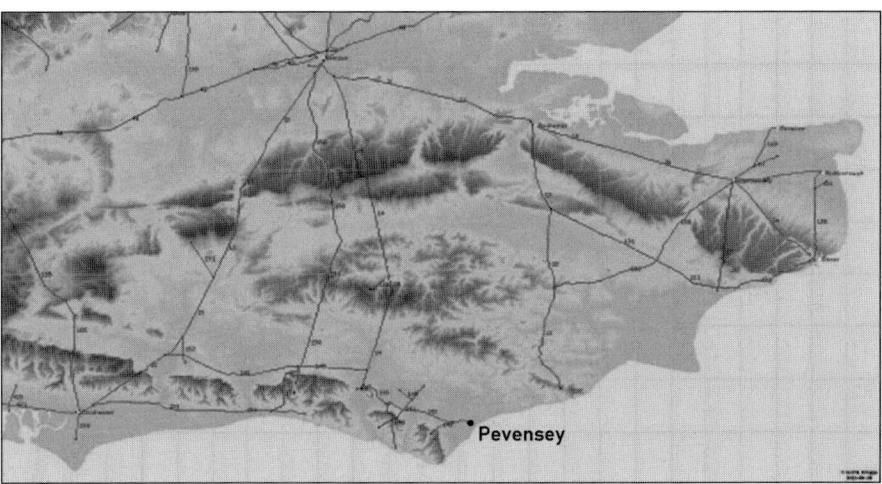

Figure 1.4 The general arrangement of Roman roads in Southeast England – Margery.

The Weald as a whole has yielded evidence of at least six Roman iron-working sites, most of which seem to have been in operation for about 200 years and the amount of slag was of the order of tens of thousands of tons. The original slag heap at the Beauport Wood

Figure 1.5 Roman agger, embankment of the road marked by a tree line near Sedlescombe.

Figure 1.6 Line of Roman Road through Sedlescombe High Street.

bloomery is said to have been well over 50,000 tons, inferring at least 25,000 tons of iron was produced in quantities of about 3–4lbs per blast from this site alone. Iron production as a whole must have far exceeded Romano-British requirements, meaning Britain was a major exporter of iron during the first few centuries of the Christian era. There would have been need for an elaborate road system out of the Weald to supply the South-East, including Canterbury, Winchester, London, and a port to ship iron out to the western Roman Empire – which Austin places where the old Port of Hastings once lay.

Chapter 2

The Saxon Port of Hastings and Norman Pre-Battle Camp

In this chapter, the task is to establish the Norman fleet's landing place following its overnight crossing of the English Channel[1] from France. Duke William of Normandy departed St Valery-sur-Somme with an army thought to be some 7,000 strong on Thursday, 28 September 1066. Arriving on the English south coast across from his point of embarkation, the duke erected his base camp, a strong defensive position against a Saxon attack, before he was ready to do battle with his adversary, King Harold II. This landing was at Hastings, an old Saxon Cinque Port, a quite different place from the modern town of Hastings just along the coast to the east. Along with the ports of Romney (Old Romney today), Dover, Sandwich and Hythe, Hastings was incorporated into the '*Confederation of Cinque Ports*'.

In exchange for certain privileges, a Cinque Port was required to provide ships and men to defend the south coast of England from the frequent seaborne attacks – other ports were incorporated later. Now, with their historic function long discontinued, the Lord Wardens who oversaw their activities are still appointed, but the title is ceremonial.

Accounts of the old port of Hastings tell us that it was one of the earliest and largest of the Cinque Ports, first operating as such in the late Saxon period, just before the Norman Conquest. But most of the original Cinque Ports have either disappeared (as with Old Hastings) or now lie inland a mile or two from the sea.

THE SAXON PORT OF HASTINGS

But since Hastings was a significant southern English port long before 1066, it seemed it might help in identifying its location if we looked into the history of the Cinque Ports. Perhaps the archives would even provide clues to the site of the Battle of Hastings itself; after all, Hastings Cinque Port must have had some involvement in the action in 1066 and it is inconceivable the event went unrecorded.

One such history, *The land of the Cinque Ports*, written and published by Petre Mais in 1949 looked promising. Unfortunately, it relates that the Cinque Ports' records prior to the thirteenth century, our period of interest, no longer existed. However, Mais' book was helpful in pointing to where the remaining Cinque Ports archives rest today. But beyond that it made clear nothing is known of the location of the ancient Saxon port of Hastings.

'Nobody knows where the old Hastings stood or whether it was Saxon, Roman or British. Nobody knows who built it. They talk of Hastea, they talk of a Roman castle and a Roman name Heastenchester. Roman pottery and iron work have been found.'

Hastings must have been an important town and port though, because Mais relates it had its own mint:

'Under the Saxons, Hastings acquired a Mint. Coins were struck here bearing the heads of Canute, Hardicanute and Edward the Confessor.'

But beyond learning that the modern town of Hastings is the fourth incarnation, the source was not helpful. So where else can we turn?

The only serious effort that has been made to discover the old Saxon town and port, as far as this writer is aware, is Nick Austin's, the results of which were published in his book, *Secrets of the Norman Invasion*, in 2012.[2]

It is unfortunate that his efforts have failed to gain much mainstream interest, but hopefully this book, by building on that work, will. Austin has worked out that the old port had been located on the banks of Combe Haven, an inland tidal water at the time of the Conquest, parts of which are at or below sea level – these wetlands are liable to flooding. The haven lies to the west of present-day Hastings and just to the south-west of the railway into Hastings (Figure 2.15). Evidence shows that the port had Roman and maybe earlier origins and was adopted by the Saxons, the Hastingas tribe, who settled locally after the end of the Roman era.

Other sources about Hastings put the old port on the coast, further to the east, beyond the first set of cliffs where modern Hastings now lies. Peter Blair in his book, *An Introduction to Anglo-Saxon England* (second edition), published in 1977, discusses the old English word '*port*', with its meaning, 'seaport', but adds that 'the word port by no means implies that the place to which it refers was situated on the coast', an important consideration when the evidence presented in this chapter is at odds with most accounts which have the Saxon port, to which the Norman fleet came, further east and on the coast itself.

The next chapter deals with Duke William's landing at the port of Hastings, but here we seek to rediscover the 'lost' Hastings by placing it on the OS map – an important step in this story.

The *Chronicle of Battle Abbey*, written in the mid-twelfth century, is a suitable starting point in this quest. It makes clear that Pevensey and its old Roman fort was not where the duke set up his base, Pevensey was but a stop on the way where he dropped off some troops. The camp was set up at Hastings:

> the duke did not long remain in that place [Pevensey], but went away with his men to a port not far distant called Hastings, where: 'he speedily built a castle of wood'.

Hechelande

The *Chronicle* next identifies the spot where the army built the castle and readied it for battle. It was at a place called Hechelande. It is clearly the army's base camp, and the place of arrival on the south coast after the fleet's Channel crossing:

THE SAXON PORT OF HASTINGS

The Norman army:

> Having arrived at a hill called Hechelande situated in the direction of Hastings, while they were helping one another on with their armour, there was brought forth a coat of mail for the duke to put on …'

So the Norman camp was at or near the point of landing, situated at Hechelande – and Hechelande was in the vicinity of the port of Hastings.

Hechelande may have been the 'Latinised' version of the local Saxon name according to how the monks heard it pronounced by the local population. Mark Anthony Lower made what is probably the first translation of the *Chronicle* from Latin into the modern English language. It was published by John Smith in 1851. Lower's translation of 'Hechelande' is a sort of reverse process, reverting to the 'Latinised' place name as he thought it might have sounded in the twelfth century.

Lower is, unsurprisingly, uncertain how best to take the monk's Latin back to Old English (OE), opting for 'Hechelande' in the main text, but offers the alternative 'Hethelande' in a footnote. No doubt scholars of Latin will understand the close relationship between the '*ch*' and the '*th*' sounds.

Now looking to match Hechelande with a named feature on the modern Hastings area map and confirm the location of the Norman camp, we found the OE word for the geographical feature, ridge,[3] is *hrycg*.[4] Adding the suffix *lande* (to match the *Chronicle*'s rendition) it becomes *hrycglande* – reasonably close-sounding to the written Hecheland, allowing leeway for monks making their own written interpretation of that spoken by local Saxons.

Anyone, as with this writer, unfamiliar with Old English with its scarcity of vowels, would find *hrycglande*, with six consecutive consonants, difficult to pronounce, so over time the '*h*' at the beginning would surely get dropped, giving us *rycglande*. Then we would not

1066: THE LOST HASTINGS BATTLEFIELD

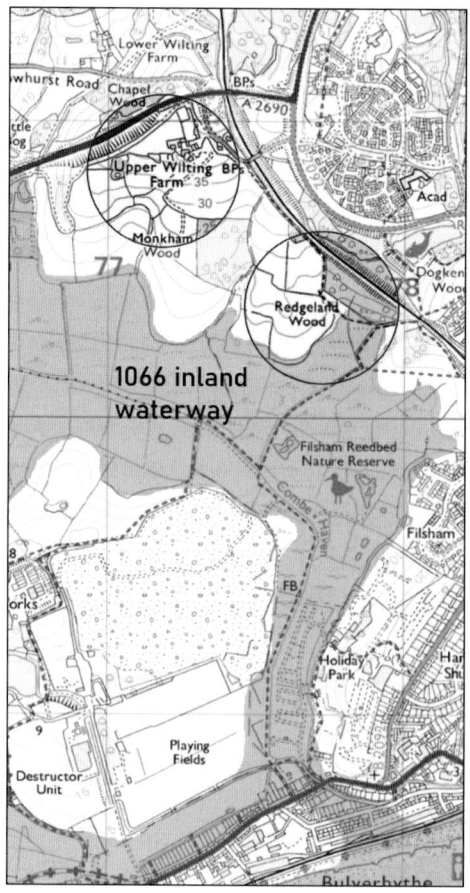

Figure 2.1 OS map (marked up) showing part of modern Hastings, and how Combe Haven as an inland waterway might have looked in 1066. See colour plate section.

be surprised that *rycglande* mutated to *ryglande*, and finally, to '*ridgeland*'. There is a named wood on the OS map of Hastings/Bexhill: 'Redgeland Wood'. Is this proof that the Hecheland described in the medieval *Chronicle* where the Normans arrived was at Redgeland Wood? – this writer recognises that this interpretation would benefit from professional etymological expertise.

Redgeland Wood lies on sloping land adjacent to Combe Haven shown on the 1:25,000 OS map, tile and grid reference TQ 777103 (Figure 2.1). The GE elevation tracing tool shows the height of the land about Redgeland Wood rising from 2m at Combe Haven basin to 15m at Redgeland Wood, some 250m distance from the haven and continuing its rise for another 200m northwards to Upper Wilting Farm. This is claimed by Austin to be the location of the old Saxon burh and site for the Norman 'upper fort' in 1066. Here the maximum elevation is 44m.

This cursory examination of Battle Abbey's 'Hechelande', and its association with the old port of Hastings and the site for the Norman landings, is not claimed to be conclusive in itself, but together with other findings in this chapter the case for it becomes quite compelling.

THE SAXON PORT OF HASTINGS

The Anglo-Saxon Burh

There were thirty-three Anglo-Saxon burhs (fortified towns or settlements) in the tenth century Saxon Burghal Hidage list. The location of the burh at Hastings, unlike the others, is not given. Here, we have sought to rectify this omission; the Hastings burh, whose location Nick Austin claims to have identified, is thought to be of Roman provenance.[5]

It is relatively small, at 500 hides, compared with most of the others. Austin has carried out extensive field work at Wilting Farm studying the ramparts and ditches. He believes Chapel Field (Figure 2.2. to 2.4) to be the site of the remains of the burh – his findings were recorded in his *Secrets of the Norman Invasion*. He has also looked further to the south along the banks of Combe Haven to try and locate the old port.

We seek here to build on this work by looking at the relationship between his field measurements and the historic burh hidage record:

> Firstly, a hide was essentially a 4ft length of wall making the 500 hide Hastings defensive burh perimeter some 2,000ft long. The aerial view of the Chapel Field burh (Figure 2.2) shows it to be approximately rectangular in shape, with, as far as can be judged, an aspect ratio of length to breadth of 6.5/4.5. From this we have calculated the area of the burh at roughly 5.5 acres.[6]

In his work at Wilting Farm, Austin has measured Chapel Field (which contains the ramparts and ditches) finding it to occupy 4.52 acres:[7]

> The top field at Wilting (Upper Wilting farm), on the very summit of the land where the manor house now stands, is called Chapel Field and is 4.52 acres.

The extent of the Hasting's burh has been calculated here from the historical record at 5.5 acres. It is in the same 'ball park' then as Austin's surveyed area of 4.52 acres. The variance of 18 per cent can perhaps be accounted for by the error created by our assumption the burh was perfectly rectangular and the rough estimation taken from the aerial view that the aspect ratio of the rectangle was 6.5/4.5. Austin's aerial photographs, Figures 2.3 and 2.4, clearly show the remains of defensive ramparts and ditches within Chapel Field.

In case it is thought the correspondence between the calculated 5.5 acres and the surveyed 4.52 acres is something of a fluke, then consider the work carried out on this subject by Richard Abels. Abels[8] at the Winchester burh notes the burh perimeter is clearly defined by the remains of the town wall unlike that at Wilting Farm:

> In some cases, the correspondence between the actual length of walls and its hidage allocation in the text is nothing short of remarkable. In the case of Winchester it is almost exact: the text's 2,400 hides allows for 3,300 yards of wall while the city's actual Roman walls extend for 3,318 yards.

Here we have added value to Austin's work, removing, we believe, any lingering doubt that the defences at Wilting Farm, one of thirty-three across southern England, were the work of Anglo-Saxons at the time these ancient burhs were being constructed against Viking incursions. The burh at Wilting Farm, though perhaps founded on previous workings (Roman for instance), are not essentially from some other time, though, as we shall see, the burh was used by William the Conqueror to protect his army after landing. Nick Austin believes the Normans had their upper camp at Wilting, utilising and reinforcing those Saxon ramparts. They were following the logic of the choice of the site made by their predecessors. Later, in Chapter 6, we look at the erection of the upper and lower forts by the Normans by the banks of Combe Haven.

THE SAXON PORT OF HASTINGS

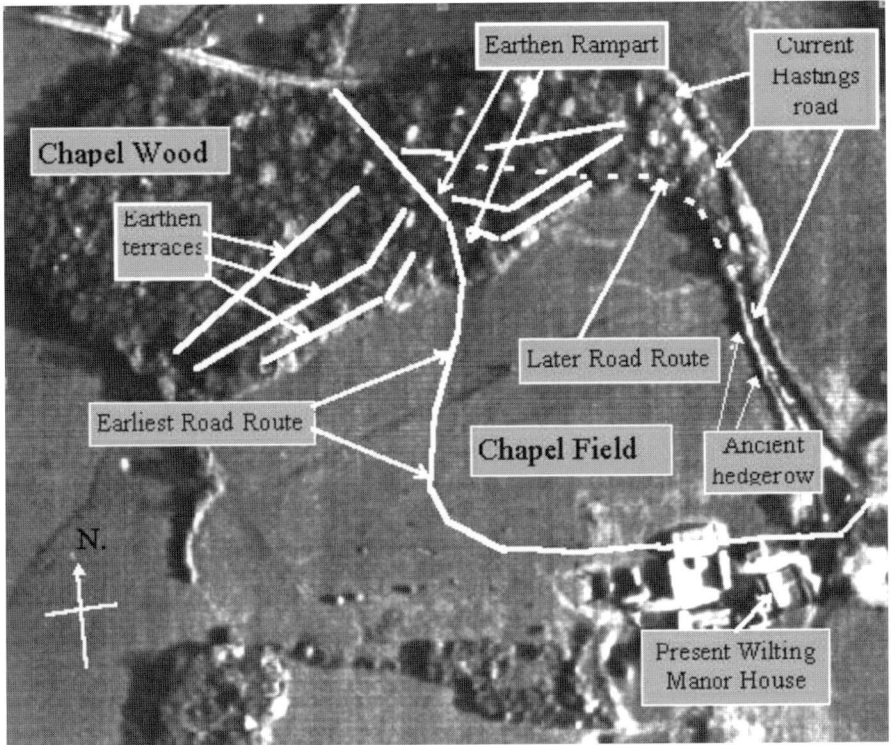

Figure 2.2 Aerial view of Upper Wilting Manor House and adjacent fields.

Figure 2.3 Northern section of rampart looking east, separating lower and higher levels of Chapel Field.

1066: THE LOST HASTINGS BATTLEFIELD

Figure 2.4 Western end of rampant looking east with the Manor House in the top right corner.

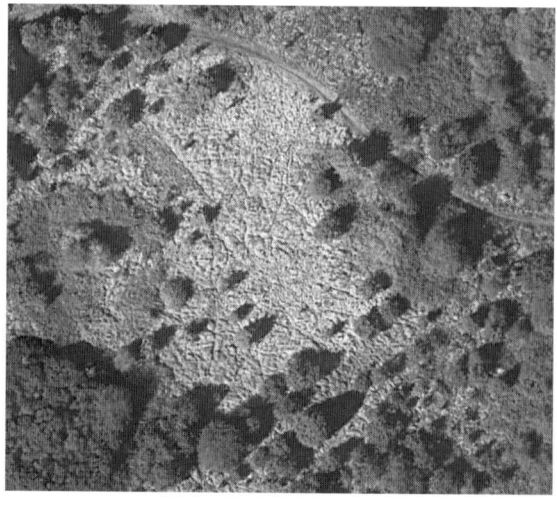

Figure 2.5 Google Earth outlines of the old Port of Hastings. See colour plate section.

We should be relieved that Nick Austin had done his work and taken the photographs of Chapel Field at Wilting Farm when he did. In 2015, East Sussex Council carved a major road through the site to connect Hastings and Bexhill (A2690), thereby obliterating, for ever, important archaeological evidence

THE SAXON PORT OF HASTINGS

in the process. Now, only a small area of the southern part of the site remains for future investigation. However, Oxford Archaeology did carry out an extensive dig prior to construction being started; the preliminary report showing potential for archaeology is now published. Details of finds made are awaiting further publication.

Now to continue the investigation. It is well known that ancient, man-made, earth disturbances not normally discernible at ground level, can, viewed from above, under favourable conditions (most often after a long hot, dry, spell), reveal tracings where old structures, roadways and other features once stood.

Recently, conditions were suitable to see signs of the destroyed old port of Hastings – these can be seen in the GE satellite picture image (Figure 2.5). It shows clearly the outlines of what must have been buildings and passages or roadways over the whole central area. But what is particularly tantalising is the pair of concentric circles' feature in the centre, together with the suggestion of what may once have been a north/south street running up to it (the circular feature) and beyond, right down to where the water once lapped the banks of Combe Haven. There is also a triangular pattern to the

Figure 2.6 St John's church, Piddinghoe, East Sussex. (credit Alamy)

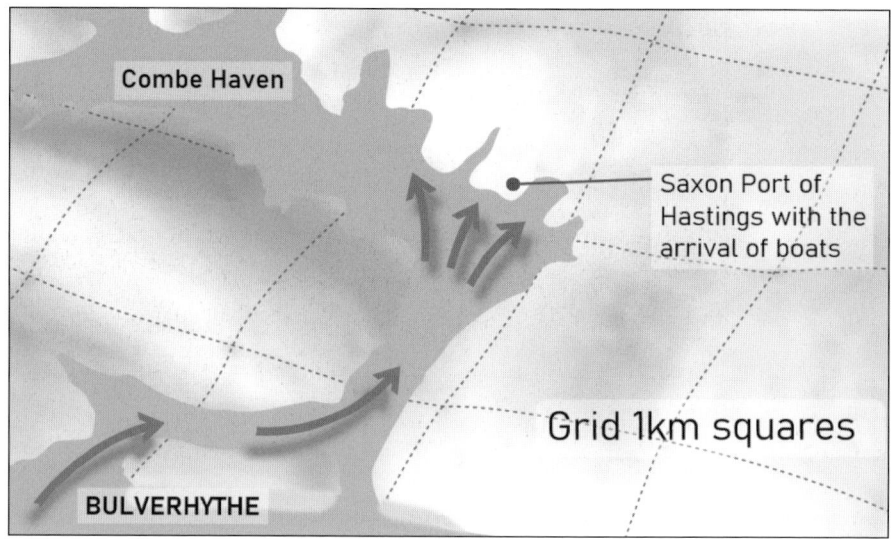

Figure 2.7 Combe Haven and its access to the sea at Bulverhythe.

Figure 2.8 Old Hastings and its port area (5m contour red line land/water boundary) as it would have been in 1066 (Google Earth).

THE SAXON PORT OF HASTINGS

Figure 2.9 St Andrew's round-tower church, East Lexham and its shadow.

north of the circular feature – its original purpose a mystery, at least until archaeological expertise can be brought to bear.

This circular feature could indicate the point where a round tower once stood; a lookout tower perhaps or a church tower or both. There were nearly a thousand round tower churches in England at one time; now there are approximately 181 remaining, including the remnants of decayed or collapsed structures. These unusual churches are only found in Norfolk (126), Suffolk (42), Essex (6), Cambridgeshire (2), all in East Anglia, Berkshire (2) and importantly for this story, three in East Sussex.

Two of these three East Sussex, Saxon, round-tower churches, St John's, Piddinghoe (Figure 2.6), which is early twelfth century and St Peter, Southease, chartered in AD 966, lie along the lower reaches of the River Ouse which flows into the English Channel at the small port of Newhaven. St Michael Church, Lewes, the third round-tower church, is further inland away from the coast.

Piddinghoe and Southease churches lie 24 miles away from the port of Hastings, near enough in distance and time to have shared a common architecture and function and most probably having a defensive role as

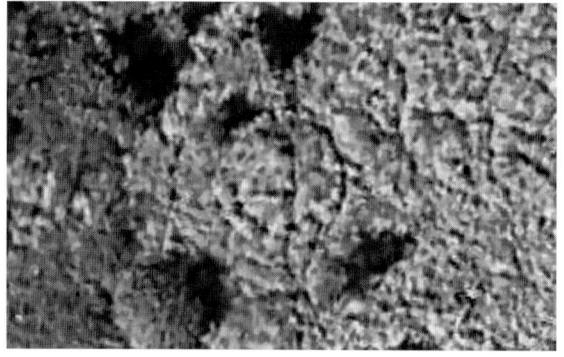

Figure 2.10 Circular feature – Google Earth.

well as an ecclesiastic purpose at the time of the Norman Conquest.

If the circular feature showing on the GE picture, Figure 2.5, and shown enlarged opposite in Figure 2.10, is the outline of a tower, what was its purpose? A watch tower or a tower abutting a church? It could have had a role in the local defences, in addition to any ecclesiastic function, an early warning system against raids along the south coast. The Vikings had been attacking Saxon England from the eighth century right up to the Norman Conquest and beyond.

The GE image (Figure 2.9) of St Andrew's Church, East Lexham, West Norfolk, is included to get a measure of the tower's diameter to

Figure 2.11 All Saints, Cockley Cley. (Thanks to the Church Warden, All Saints, Cockley Cley)

allow comparison with the diameter of the circular feature already cited at Hastings. St Andrew's church tower is 19ft in diameter, a figure obtained from Google Earth. Measurements have also been made in the same way at Piddinghoe (16ft) and Southease (14ft) towers. The enlarged image of the circular feature (Figure 2.10 above) at Hastings, at 18ft across, matches the dimension of St Andrew's church tower, qualifying it as a contender for inclusion in the list of the 1,000 English round-tower churches that once graced southeastern England. Furthermore, the ruined church at Cockley Cley, (Figure 2.11), reveals the solidity of its construction with its very thick walls. It is useful to make a comparison of the cross-sectional view of the wall exposed at Cockley, with that of the GE circular feature at the port of Hastings. We can see in Figure 2.10, a concentric ring-like impression marking, presumably, below ground debris from the demolished tower – the outer and inner tracings of a wall. Note how neatly the picture (Figure 2.11) and satellite image (Figure 2.10) dimensions compare.

If the tower had once functioned as a lookout tower, it would need to have been high enough to give sight of the seascape from its top. The view of the sea from ground level at what we consider was once the port of Hastings was mostly obstructed, only being in view in very limited directions, because Bulverhythe, right on the coast, blocked the line of sight to the sea. Today, Bulverhythe carries the Hastings–Bexhill A259 road and railway line. The terrain at Bulverhythe at its highest elevation is 32m (104ft), including buildings. Allowing 20ft for the height of modern buildings, 15ft land elevation at the circular feature, and 6ft for the height of the lookout man, the tower would, we have calculated, needed to be a little over 60ft in height for the seascape to be visible in a southerly direction. Considering that some churches today boast round towers of about 60ft height, with St Peter's at Brampton, Suffolk being 72ft and St Andrew's round church tower at Hasketon a lofty 90ft, it is not fanciful to postulate a tower at the port of Hastings high enough to be part of an early alert network

Figure 2.12 Artist's impression of the medieval port of Hastings at Combe Haven – John Tucker. See colour plate section.

THE SAXON PORT OF HASTINGS

at the time of the Battle of Hastings.

What does all this mean? It means that if we accept the circular feature shown on the satellite map at the old port of Hastings is an archaeological feature, then the area delineated in Figure 2.5 at the eastern extremity of Combe Haven was a town of some size, sporting a tall masonry tower with, most likely, an attached church as well. That the port of Hastings was destroyed at the Conquest and never rebuilt (refer to Chapter 6) means that the mystery of its location is resolved, subject to archaeological confirmation.

Figure 2.13 Track out of Crowhurst Park (south of) that may once have been a Roman route from the bloomery in Beauport Park to port of Old Hastings.

The Road to Hastings

Here we are looking for signs of roads – if there are no roads, then there cannot have been the port of Hastings on the banks of Combe Haven. Nick Austin has, as we have related earlier, carried out an extensive study of the many tracks around the port site area, and in his *Secrets of the Norman Invasion* describes two tracks leading to the bloomeries in what are now known as Beauport Park and Blackhorse Hill.

It is believed that the Beauport bloomery, in the thickly wooded area of several square miles extent, was being worked before the Romans came to Britain and the OS map of the area confirms Roman activity, marking the location of the Roman Bloomery.

Figure 2.14 What looks like Roman trackway to the bloomery site off the A2100 road by 'The Mount'.

We have already seen this bloomery was very important to the Roman Empire, credited with being the third largest. But notwithstanding Austin's findings, there would have, of necessity, had to be a suitable load-bearing road, or roads, connecting the Beauport Wood bloomery to the port for onward shipment of heavy iron ore or smelted products to the continent and also from the bloomery inland to meet the needs of the Province for iron. The very presence of this foremost bloomery at Beauport Wood implies the existence of an integrated road system and port in Roman times.

That the bloomery was still being worked until the early days of the Industrial Revolution in the nineteenth century, when purer ores were being discovered elsewhere in the country, means iron was almost certainly being extracted at Beauport Wood (and surrounding sites) through the centuries and without doubt at the time of the Conquest. The local road network in 1066, although probably not then being maintained to high Roman standards, would have been available for Duke William's and King Harold's armies.

Viewing roads and tracks marked on pre-railway maps of the area, freeing us from the problem of cluttered modern maps filled with the proliferation of roads, buildings and other information, we can see there are several possible ways from the Roman bloomery to the port

THE SAXON PORT OF HASTINGS

of Hastings. One leading from the port northwards, through the dip just to the east of the burh at Wilting Farm, sweeps west, then northwards to Blackhorse Hill, where there was likely another bloomery (Austin writes of one), and on into Beauport Wood to the Roman bloomery. The case for this route is strengthened by the route's passing of the water tower and Mount (see later chapter) on the A2100, and running (Figure 2.15) through the woodlands and to the bloomery site and beyond. It looks Roman in origin and therefore the best candidate for the port link. It would have been there at the Conquest. It links up with Roman Kent Street (A21) on the northern side of Beauport Park woodland and is the obvious entry point for Harold's army marching south giving cover for the assembly of troops before it rushed forward to take control of the battle site – see Chapter 9.

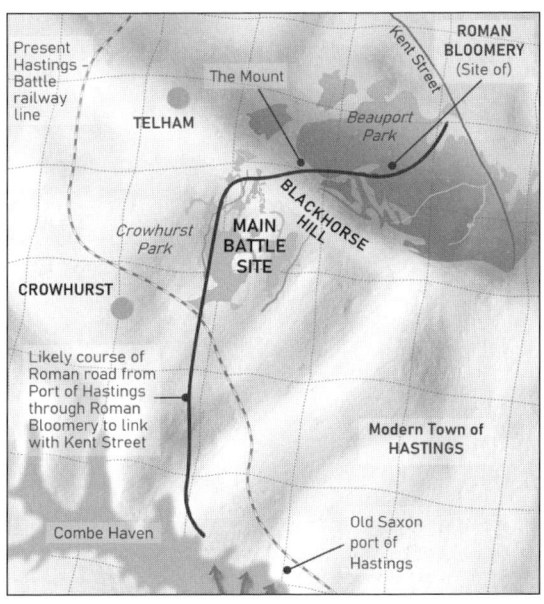

Figure 2.15 Topographical map showing the 1066 inland waterway, the area's relief and the relationship of Blackhorse Hill battle site to the old Saxon port of Hastings.

In walking the route from the port site to Blackhorse Hill, occasional pieces of what looked like smelted iron (bloom) were lying on the track up to the Hill (Figure 2.13). As we have noted, iron-working was still going on in East Sussex into the nineteenth century; expert examination might confirm this and when it was produced.

So here we have ample evidence for a Saxon defensive burh at Wilting Farm, the Hastings port site co-located just to the south, as well as a developed, if not up to Roman standards, network of local roads and tracks connected to the rest of the country. Generally, access inland from the south-east coast of England was difficult, with poorly drained low-lying marshlands and large expanses of inland waterways interspersed with inaccessible cliffs. There were few ports with easy access inland to London. The port at Hastings and its developed hinterland up to the Saxon burh was, with Rye and Dover, an exception. Hastings was the closest of the ports to London and provided one of the shortest crossings for the Norman fleet assembled at St Valery, an important factor at a time when sea voyaging was extremely hazardous. The rapidity of the Saxon army's march to confront the invader demonstrates the quality of the road network leading south from Stamford Bridge in Yorkshire to Hastings.

In Chapters 5 and 6, we see how the historical accounts describing the foothold gained at the old port of Hastings after Duke William landed fit well with the geography of the area occupied. The Battle of Hastings, fought on 14 October, was now just fourteen days away.

Chapter 3

Saxon and Norman Strategic Considerations

There were three claimants to the English throne at the death of the childless Edward the Confessor on 5 January 1066: Earl Harold Godwinson, the most powerful figure in the kingdom; William Duke of Normandy; and the Norwegian king, Harald Hardrada. William alleged that King Edward had promised him the throne on his death and one version of the story is that Edward had earlier sent Harold to Normandy to confirm his promise to him. However, on his deathbed Edward named Harold his successor. The truth will never be known.

Few writers have commented on William's good fortune in making a safe, unopposed landing, but one wonders whether chance was at play or strategic planning was behind it. The English fleet and most of the land defences had been disbanded, we are told, due to the pressing need to gather in the harvest. Then the Norwegian king, aided by Harold's rebellious brother, Tostig, had invaded in the north – causing the English king to march his army to oppose him and leaving the south coast largely undefended.

Accounts, mostly favourable to Duke William, have the Norman fleet holed up in St Valery awaiting better weather, but there remains the suspicion that the true reason for the delay was to await the expected departure of the English army north. Surely, William was well aware of the strength of Harold's army, demonstrated by its success at Stamford Bridge on Monday, 25 September, four days before William sailed. William would have been wary of a strongly opposed amphibious landing; his best hope, perhaps his only hope, was collaboration with the Norwegian king, a fellow Norseman.

It has been thought that William offered Harold a choice between single combat,[1] in a pre-Hastings battle parley, or division of the kingdom between them, rather than have the two armies face mass slaughter. The duke, perhaps expecting to split the kingdom with Harald Hardrada had, after the Norwegian king's unexpected defeat and death, offered the same split to Harold. Whether wind conditions prior to William sailing actually delayed him or whether William was waiting for Harold's departure north leaving the coast virtually undefended, is not stated in Norman accounts and the discovery of independent documents clearing up the matter is unlikely. This will have to remain speculation, but it does not affect the mission to discover the site of the Battle of Hastings.

Before taking his army north, *The Carmen*[2] account suggests Harold had taken some basic precautions by leaving lookouts behind on the coast to report any Norman landing and who would then rush north to inform Harold:

> One of the English, lying hidden close to a sea rock, perceived how the countless ranks spread far and wide and saw the fields glitter, full of glancing arms. He saw the people, their homes ravaged by flames for their perfidy [*sic*][3] by the raging sword, and what tears the children shed for their fathers' slaughter. He ran to mount a horse and sped to tell the king.

Wace has much the same story but with the Englishman being described as a knight and the sea-rock, a hill. No doubt this 'Englishman' was stationed there to watch out for and report the expected invasion when it was sighted. The slaughter of the innocent population and destruction wrought to their homes is understood by some historians to have been perpetrated to enrage the king and coerce him into taking pre-emptive action to save the

SAXON AND NORMAN STRATEGIC CONSIDERATIONS

land from further devastation; land, much of which was held by the king personally. But instead of adopting a more prudent course by resting his depleted forces after the Stamford Bridge battle, gathering more men and waiting for the enemy to come to him, Harold reacted to the provocation and sped south. Perhaps he felt, after his dramatic victory, confident of repeating his success, after all he was on home ground and delaying would of course have led to more destruction.

It was a difficult but fateful decision for an island's history. Yes, delay meant the invader might have reinforced his army from France, but not necessarily so (at this stage there was less incentive to join William than after the Battle of Hastings was won). The Norman boats were quite small, open and hastily constructed. Winter was fast approaching and October could bring gales in the Channel that would cut off supplies and block retreat. Even if William was able to persuade his allies to dispatch more troops, transporting them over might have been impossible. If William were to take the kingdom, he would be forced to act soon and marching his army inland to confront Harold's army was one of his options. But if Harold held back, starvation, disease and ambush as the Normans struggled through the heavily wooded countryside of southern England would have led to slow attrition and eventual annihilation. If they had managed to escape back to their longships, the Saxon fleet would have been waiting for them. William's ruthless strategy of burning and plundering had worked.

Before leaving Sussex at the end of the summer to confront the Norwegian king, accounts indicate that Harold took further precautions against an invasion whilst away by depriving William of the fortifications at Hastings by destroying them. The Bishop of Amiens' *The Carmen* implies this in the continuation of his account:

> You [Duke William] restored the dismantled forts which stood there formerly and set custodians to hold them.

We do not need to dwell too long on this, as it has but limited bearing on the subject of the site of the Battle of Hastings and those wishing for a deeper understanding can refer to Nick Austin's *Secrets of the Norman Invasion* where he discusses the obscurity surrounding who it was that destroyed the forts (and the town): William or Harold. And *The Carmen* fails to clarify the matter but its words: 'Fearing to lose the ships, you [William] surrounded them with earthworks …' is consistent with William's army settling on the banks of Combe Haven at and about the old port of Hastings, preparing for the coming battle.

Chapter 4

Did the Normans Land at Pevensey or Hastings?

Along with many of this writer's generation educated in the epic story of the Battle of Hastings, schoolchildren learned that the Norman duke, known as William the Conqueror, landed his fleet of longships at Pevensey, East Sussex, after crossing from France. There, he set up his military encampment amongst the ruins of the large Roman fortress, where his army was prepared for the battle he had come to fight. Then, on 14 October, 1066, the army marched northward, fought and defeated the English army at the Battle of Hastings when the last Saxon king, Harold, was slain by an arrow in the eye following a volley from Norman archers.

We may have understood the battle to have taken place at Battle Abbey in the post-battle town of Battle, but knew it as the Battle of Hastings. It was never explained to us why a battle fought some 9 miles distant from another supposedly unrelated town, Hastings, should be called that. When the battle first came to be known as the Battle of Hastings is difficult to determine, but that 'Hastings' is the appropriate name for the battle will become clear as this story told here unfolds.

But did William land his army at Pevensey? When the historical texts are examined, it soon becomes apparent that the movements of Duke William's fleet after first approaching the English side of the Channel are anything but clear. With accounts often contradictory and confusing, it would not have been surprising if those scribe-monks trying to make sense of events, were as confused as modern historians – but did their best anyway.

1066: THE LOST HASTINGS BATTLEFIELD

Unfortunately, writers[1] about the battle have been constrained against approaching the history with a broader mind by the overwhelming obstacle presented against a deeper investigation of the Battle of Hastings by Battle Abbey having supposedly been built on the 1066 battlefield to commemorate the battle and remember the dead. As we shall see later, the monks, for reasons of their own, probably let it be thought the abbey had been constructed on the field of battle and the tradition was established from the beginning. It seems to have outweighed other considerations, particularly that a large Norman army with hundreds of horses, and no doubt wheeled transport, would have found it virtually impossible to skirt the Pevensey levels around the banks of the area of wetlands liable to flooding now known as Combe Haven and cross impenetrable marshland to the Battle Abbey site. Yet some accounts still persist in having the army setting off from Pevensey[2] on that fateful October morning.

When the duke sailed from St Valery, it is inconceivable that he left without a clear plan for where he was heading and what he was going to do when he arrived. That meant he needed a sound knowledge of the landing area and its hinterland in general. During more than twenty years preceding the invasion, Edward the Confessor, who had spent his formative years in Normandy before ascending to the English throne in 1042, favoured Normans with positions as counsellors, churchmen and military leaders. Edward even appointed William of Jumièges to the highest church post in the land as Archbishop of Canterbury. His brother-in-law, the Count of Boulogne, joined his court in 1051 and Ralph the Timid, son of Norman Count of Vexin, was appointed Earl of Hereford. William, through these Norman aristocrats at the centre of the English establishment, would have learned of the geography of the southern coastal area and the strengths and weaknesses of landing points for an army.

William might even have heard of the near disaster a millennium before when the Romans attempted their first invasions of Britain.

DID THE NORMANS LAND AT PEVENSEY OR HASTINGS?

Julius Caesar invading in 55 BC and being used to the calmer waters of the Mediterranean, instead of seeking a safe haven, beached the fleet by the sea or left them riding at anchor. When the next inevitable storm hit, boats filled with water or those riding at anchor were driven against each other. Many were wrecked and others rendered unseaworthy, threatening the return to the continent when defeated by the local tribes. Much the same happened the following year when they invaded again, not having learned the lessons from the previous year. This time, they suffered considerable damage, losing about forty ships.

But William, familiar with Channel conditions, knew better, and with intelligence gleaned from his contacts in England, the port of Hastings would have been earmarked as the best landing place for the bulk of the army. Hastings, with its relatively easy access to the capital was ideal and William might have been advised against landing further to the west where he risked dispersal and loss of ships[3] on the longer sea crossing. Although he was probably unaware the Saxon fleet had already left,[4] he wanted to limit any risk of encountering Harold's patrolling ships. Disembarking further east, London was more distant and the coast, mostly cliffs or marshland, lacked suitable landing places for his large fleet – about 700 longboats.[5] Though Wace, alone of the accounts, has Hastings being the first landfall, other accounts agree the first landfall, following a moonless night crossing, was Pevensey, where, according to Florence of Worcester, he ordered the fleet to drop anchor: 'he had moored his fleet at a place called Pevensey', presumably to allow stragglers to catch up and assemble his forces before disembarking.

Both William of Jumièges and William of Poitiers have similar stories,[6] relating that the landing was unopposed and Pevensey seized, fortified and garrisoned – securing the duke's left flank. The accounts continue with William moving on to Hastings, which is also fortified, whilst 'some split from the main group and come ashore at Romney',[7] forming the army's right (eastern) defensive flank further along the coast.

The *Chronicle of Battle Abbey* confirms this, having the duke arrive 'safely near the castle called Pevensey' and, 'the duke did not long remain in that place [Pevensey], but went away with his men to a port not far distant called Hastings' where 'he speedily built a castle of wood'.

The *Anglo-Saxon Chronicle* ('D' version) is also consistent with this: 'Then William earl [duke] of Normandy came to Pevensey on the eve of the Feast of St. Michael' [Friday, 29 September].[8] 'And as soon as they were able to move on, they erected a stronghold at Hastings', then the 'E' version completes the landings with: 'Earl [Duke] William landed at Hastings on Michaelmass day' [Saturday, 30 September]. Henry of Huntingdon's account, short on facts, simply states the duke 'landed on the south coast, and had built a fort at Hastings'.

The Carmen mentions only a single landing, without naming or dating it, simply stating the fleet[9] arrived at 'safe landing-places, leaving the sea astern, the third hour of day[10] was rising over the earth'. The 'safe landing-places' and 'leaving the sea astern', is consistent with a landing in Combe Haven.

Then, after relating the destruction of the English as foretold by a comet,[11] *The Carmen* continues: 'Robbed of her terrified inhabitants, the land destined for you [the duke] joyfully received you and yours in a calm bay.' This must also be referring to the second landing place, the 'calm bay' being the inland waterway, now the reclaimed wetlands known as Combe Haven – we have argued previously that this second and main landing place cannot have been anywhere else. It is clear from all this, that it was Hastings where the Norman army landed and, from our earlier study, Hastings was located on the banks of Combe Haven.

Naturally, as the well-known adage has it, an army marches on its stomach and any supplies brought from France needed to be supplemented with what could be taken from the surrounding countryside. Wace colourfully describes the Norman army's frenzied

DID THE NORMANS LAND AT PEVENSEY OR HASTINGS?

activity, including scorching the land on arriving; we can do no better than relate it here:

> They arrived near Hastings, and there each ship ranged side by side. There you might see the good sailors, the serjeants [*sic*] and squires sally forth and unload the ships; cast the anchors, haul the ropes bear out shields and saddles, and land the warhorses and palfreys [saddle horses]. The archers came forth, and touched land the foremost; each with his bow bent, and his quiver full of arrows slung at his side. … All stood well equipped, and in good courage to fight; and they scoured the whole shore, but found not an armed man there. After the archers had gone forth, the knights landed next, all armed; with their hauberks [chain mail tunic] on, their shields slung round their necks, and their helmets laced.
>
> They formed together on the shore, each armed upon his war horse. All had their swords girded on, and passed into the plain with their lances raised.

Wace, unfortunately, fails to tell us precisely where this happened, leaving it 'near Hastings' – writing so long after the event, he probably did not actually know. The account, although contradicting others over which landing came first, Pevensey or Hastings,[12] is one of the most informative accounts of this phase of the story, showing that Wace must have been in touch with knowledgeable informants. From the account, we learn a little about the topography at the landing area. We can conclude from it that with all the activity involved in the disembarkment, the army, many thousands strong and landing with horses and supplies, could not have completed it in the single day it did (30 September), below the lofty cliffs where modern-day Hastings and the ruins of the later Norman castle at West Hill now lie. The beach below these cliffs would, as today, have been sloping down to the sea and shingle-covered, and with amphibious landings being notoriously hazardous and troops at their most vulnerable, any prudent commander would not have contemplated it. Furthermore, a beach landing would have necessitated ships being dragged to the top of the cliffs, a huge effort for no good reason: a beach landing, as presumed by some authors, would not have happened.

The army that 'passed into the plain with their lances raised' is describing a landing around the shores of the inland sea behind Bulverhythe – Combe Haven.

Attempting a beach landing further east along the coast beyond the cliffs would have been no easier. Yes, the ground would have been level, but would have been marshy in 1066 and even more distant than Combe Haven from the battle site. As we shall see later, too distant to reach in time for a battle (recorded as) beginning at nine o'clock in the morning.

Chapter 5

How was the Fleet Disposed After Landing?

We saw in Chapter 2 that Hastings port lay within the bounds of Combe Haven,[1] that it was Duke William's chosen landing place and that it would have made no sense, as some accounts have it, beaching his vessels on the foreshore under the cliffs to the east, risking destruction from storms or attack from Harold's navy. In addition to the shelter and security he knew Combe Haven offered, William would have been aware of the adjacent rising ground prior to setting sail, and made necessary preparations to use it for the army's base camp, so his forces could prepare for the coming battle and more easily meet any Saxon attack in the meantime.

The most realistic estimate of a 700-ship fleet[2] and allowing 20ft shore space per ship, it would have taken up some 2½ miles of bank space along the haven.[3] Combe Haven in 1066 with its many inlets and bays would have been an attractive landing place for a fleet of this size. The ships, however, were probably less concentrated than that, as some of the

Figure 5.1 HIC EXEUNT CABALLI DE NAVIBUS – Here the horses leave the ship.

fleet would have been left at Romney and Pevensey with the flanking forces so they could communicate with Hastings. Others would have been anchored or tethered on the banks of the haven ready for immediate deployment in defence of the camp and the transportation of raiding parties. Many ships would have been dragged further up the bank to minimise dispersal and then we have accounts of boats being burned or 'earthed up'. The Bayeux Tapestry shows a defensive motte being dug and the spoil piled up against an upturned longship.

In fact, written sources differ widely as to the deployment, with the *Chronicle of Battle Abbey* having them destroyed:

> having burnt the greatest part of his ships (lest any of his followers, relying on the hope of returning home ...).

But William of Poitiers and *The Carmen* are in agreement, telling us that Duke William was fearful of losing his ships so built ramparts and ditches to protect them and his men from attack, William of Poitiers writing that the fortifications were 'to serve as a defence both for themselves and for their ships', and *The Carmen* 'Fearing to lose the ships, you [Duke William] surrounded them with earthworks and guarded the shores', causes us to question the Battle Abbey account of the greater part of his ships being deliberately burned.

We shall see in a later chapter that the monks forged many documents to strengthen their claim to special privileges. Doubts over the motives of the authors of the *Chronicle of Battle Abbey* have meant this book has had to treat the *Chronicle* with special care when using it as evidence of the course of events.

Although the Norman army had long been expected, it must have come as a tremendous shock when at last it arrived, a vast sea of sails, weapons glistening, and although no account records it, accompanied perhaps by the threatening beat of drums. The inhabitants may have become complacent as September rolled on and no fleet sighted.

HOW WAS THE FLEET DISPOSED AFTER LANDING?

Wace describes the reaction when it finally arrived on the last day of September:

> A knight of that country [a Saxon knight] heard the noise and cry made by the peasants and villains when they saw the Normans were come, and that their object was to seize the land. He posted himself behind a hill, so that they [the Normans] should not see him, and tarried there, watching the arrival of the great fleet. He saw the archers come forth from the ships, and the knights follow. He saw carpenters with axes, and the host of people and troops. He saw the men throw the materials for the fort out of the ships. He saw them build up and enclose the fort, and dig the fosse around it.

A Saxon 'posting himself behind a hill' is incompatible with a main landing at Pevensey, where the terrain is flat. And although we are treating the *Chronicle of Battle Abbey* with caution, it is worth quoting it again, there is no contradiction with other accounts and, importantly, the stated place of arrival has been identified already as a recognisable present-day feature: 'Having arrived at a hill called Hechelande situated in the direction of Hastings', where Hechelande, we have argued, is Redgeland Wood by the banks of Combe Haven on OS maps. *The Carmen*, as we have seen, tells us the population fled as soon as the longships appeared, the land being 'robbed of their terrified inhabitants'.

William then set about re-using the remains of the fortification at Hastings, presumably destroyed by King Harold in his scorched-earth policy, after he'd released men guarding the shores to gather in the harvest and taken others north to do battle with the Norwegians. *The Carmen* tells us:

> You [William] restored the dismantled forts which had stood there formerly and set custodians to hold them.

The Wastings

Wastings is the term taken from the *Domesday Book* to describe the towns and villages destroyed and made worthless by the sacking carried out either before the battle or after the victory as the vengeful army took retribution.

The *Anglo-Saxon Chronicle* records the events from their perspective:

> When the earl [duke] came to England he began to plunder, and take possession of the land as he came along.

Figure 5.2 *HIC DOMUS INCENDITUR* – Here a house is burned.

HOW WAS THE FLEET DISPOSED AFTER LANDING?

and *The Carmen*, written from the Norman perspective, has the same grim account:

> Having gained control, though over no great space, your people attacked the region, laid it to waste, and burnt it with fire.

These events are dramatically illustrated in the Bayeux Tapestry image Figure 5.2, and the accompanying caption in Latin, *HIC DOMUS INCENDITUR* needs no translation. The terrified woman and child, shown here fleeing the stylish two-storey dwelling being torched by two Norman soldiers might well have been in the Hastings area. The colourful robes indicate high-status people. The extent of the destruction visited upon the East Sussex landscape is illustrated in the map in Appendix 4.

The *Chronicle of Battle Abbey*, in line with other accounts, would have had no axe to grind when it tells us the duke, 'anxiously hastened to reduce the surrounding country'.

Chapter 6

Erecting the Upper and Lower Forts at Hastings

Michael Lawson in his book, *Battle of Hastings*, first published in 2003, acknowledges that a 'bridgehead' was established at Hastings by the invading Normans and that Hastings in 1066 was a town with its own mint and may have had effective defensive ramparts with its own garrison. But the book provides no clues to the whereabouts of Hastings, or that Hastings was a port, one of the Cinque Ports.

Since Lawson's book was published, Nick Austin has described in *Secrets of the Norman Invasion*, the extensive surveys he conducted over 120 acres or so of ground gently rising from south-east to north-west on the banks of Combe Haven. Austin believes the area accommodated both the upper and the lower forts erected by Duke William after landing.

Austin's surveys ranged from ground surveys, including some tentative excavation work, aerial lidar and ground resistivity surveys. The images showed some interesting markings hard for the inexpert to interpret and although not examined by archaeological professionals, when considered as a whole, indicate that considerable human activity may have taken place over the centuries. At the north-western end, the considerable number of embankments and ditches[1] indicate defensive works and iron workings almost certainly going back to the Iron Age. These were sequentially occupied by Romans, Saxons and in 1066, the Norman army. Wilting Farm (at the north-western end) on the site of an old manor house probably means the site has been in continuous occupation for over two millennia.

ERECTING THE UPPER AND LOWER FORTS AT HASTINGS

Though we know of no direct archaeological evidence for Saxon occupation, Wilting Farm, or more specifically the rampart-scarred area enclosing Chapel Field (refer to Chapter 2) today, is almost certainly the location of the old Hastings Saxon burh, one of the thirty-three built across Wessex to protect populations against Viking attacks. These burhs were constructed at the instigation of King Alfred the Great and built in the late ninth century or after his death in the following century. The case for it being one of the Saxon burhs has already been made in Chapter 2.

That the burh was constructed about 130 years before the Norman invasion, means it was probably still in a good state of repair in 1066. This, together with the port of Hastings lower down the slope, looks like it would have been one of the 'dismantled forts [King Harold's 'scorched earth' policy before leaving for the North of England] which had stood there formerly'[2] and which William 'restored' after disembarkation of his troops.

The first fort (the lower fort), constructed some ¾ of a mile to the south-east of the upper fort, lies on the banks of Combe Haven, on a bulge of land jutting into the haven[3] (built on the demolished port area). Austin's survey has discovered post holes placed in an irregularly shaped seven-sided figure and he believes these remains mark the location of the supports for the prefabricated fort brought over from France. That a prefabricated fort was erected is recorded by Wace in relating that a '[Saxon] knight of the country' ... 'saw carpenters with axes, and the host of people and troops. He saw the men throw the materials for the fort out of the ships. He saw them build up and enclose the fort, and dig the fosse [ditch] around it.'

Transporting a prefabricated fort that could be quickly assembled immensely reduced the time the army lay disorganised and vulnerable to attack after landing. Wace continues with his account telling us the erection was completed on the same day they arrived, 30 September:

> Then they cast out of the ships the material, and drew them
> to land, all shaped framed and pierced to receive pins which

they had brought, cut and ready in large barrels; so that before evening had well set in, they had finished a fort.

Wace, whether he realised it or not, was describing the construction of the wooden 'castle', as accounts sometimes call it, at Hastings.

And the *Anglo-Saxon Chronicle* (ASC), written from the defeated side's point of view, says much the same thing, that 'soon after his [William's] landing was effected ... they erected a castle at the port of Hastings.'

William of Jumièges is also in accord with this, having a fortress built at Hastings:

> crossing the sea he [Duke William] landed at Pevensey, ... and with others he hurried to Hastings where he erected another similar fortress.

That the work was completed in just one day sounds remarkable and it is, but then there was a whole army on hand to do it. It also speaks well of the engineering skills available to the duke, that the kit came together so smoothly – no doubt it had been assembled and disassembled in France to test it before leaving and, as with any good general, nothing had been left to chance.

So what land had William committed the army to occupy until he had to fight the inevitable battle? We have previously estimated that the ground, gently rising north-westwards from the point of disembarkation, although hemmed in by water on one side and Redgeland (Hechelande) Wood and a ridge on the other, offered sufficient space for the 7,000 troops thought to have been carried over, as well as space for the estimated 1,000 war horses forming the cavalry arm. Though quite cramped, the area was not so great as to make it impossible to speedily excavate the necessary ditches and ramparts required to supplement the pre-existing earthworks. The marshalling area, approximately rectangular in shape, was of some 120 acres extent. The section of the OS map in Figure 2.1 shows

ERECTING THE UPPER AND LOWER FORTS AT HASTINGS

Upper Wilting Farm and Redgeland Wood. These two features and the area between (to the south-west of the present-day railway line) delineate the area.

Although, as we shall see in Chapter 9, it did not work out that way, the extensive preparations William made showed he was expecting to fight a defensive battle, rather than heading north to take on the Saxons in open combat. Moving inland, cut off from supplies and reinforcements from Normandy, William would have been faced with the wasting of his army from starvation, illness and, no doubt, surprise harassing attacks launched from the heavily wooded Sussex countryside.

Instead, he would, and did, 'dig in', awaiting the return south of the English king with his exhausted and depleted army following the bloody battle at Stamford Bridge, a few days earlier – William must surely have been aware of the Norwegian king's landing in Yorkshire. Combe Haven was an ideal defensive location for the duke with its quays and moorings along the banks of the tranquil waters of the Hastings basin.

In the days leading up to the confrontation, Duke William would have been preoccupied with strengthening defences, training troops and providing for their needs. Armies, especially medieval armies, tended to live off the land they occupied – they had little choice but to plunder the land for whatever they could find. William's army would have been no different and the limited number of ships available to him would have been mainly deployed transporting soldiers, boats' crews and horses. No doubt these raiding parties would have also been on the look-out for signs of enemy troop movements and any other intelligence they could acquire. Perhaps they were in touch with Normans already living in England, Normans encouraged to emigrate by Edward the Confessor to occupy important positions. And if they had not already been deported by Harold,[4] they would have been an important source of information for William, perhaps even passing on knowledge of his opponent's journey back south.

With any spare space in the ships taken up by the prefabricated fort, it is doubtful there was much room for provisions for soldiers and fodder for horses beyond their immediate needs. The army, as we have seen, depended on ravaging the countryside to maintain itself. In addition, by attacking Harold's personal domain (Harold was a big land holder, especially in East Sussex), accounts show William hoped to draw him into an early battle – instead of facing likely defeat if he moved inland to confront Harold's army. Landing at the Hastings port area, William faced the largely undefended townspeople and was able to drive them out, take their food and whatever else they wanted. Contemporary sources have described the pillaging and the event is graphically illustrated in the Bayeux Tapestry, as noted in the previous chapter.

Evidence from The Bayeux Tapestry

The first panel, Figure 6.1, from the tapestry shows William and other leaders of the Norman army sitting down to enjoy a well-earned meal after the prefabricated fort had been erected. The second panel, Figure 6.2, shows ramparts being excavated with earth thrown up on to what appears to be an upturned longship, which use would have hastened completion of the works. The *Chronicle of Battle Abbey* says the duke 'speedily build a castle of wood',[5] wood carried over with the fleet from France. The caption on the second panel describes the

Figure 6.1 This panel shows a section of the finished pre-fabricated fort and a meal being served and consumed. Duke William and his half-brothers, Bishop Odo and Robert are among the diners.

ERECTING THE UPPER AND LOWER FORTS AT HASTINGS

completed work as a castle (*CEASTRA*). The final panel, Figure 6.3, depicts a length of wall with corner towers.

The tapestry captions do not discriminate between upper and lower forts, but Wace relates that 'the duke sat down to eat, and the barons and knights had food aplenty' and the dining took place when the fort was 'finished before evening had well set in', making the scene of this event the completed lower fort. Some figures sitting around the table have been identified as William and his half-brothers, Bishop Odo and Robert.

The second image must also be of the lower fort where the longship is shown being

Figure 6.2 *CEASTRA. ISTE JUSSIT UT FODERETUR CASTELLUM AT HESTENGA* – He ordered that a motte should be dug at Hastings.

'earthed up' to form part of the defensive ramparts. It is unlikely that longships would have been dragged three-quarters of a mile to where the upper fort was restored.

The third tapestry image is more problematic. What registers, on a first impression, is how grandiose the castle, or fortress, as it is variously called, looks. The towers and interconnecting walls seem robust and finished in more than a utilitarian style. Could the panel be showing *The Carmen*'s 'restored dismantled fort'? This seems possible as there are block-like features depicted making up one of the tower's walls and the other tower is neatly roofed over with tiles. This is quite an elaborate structure, begging the question as to whether the structure was still partially standing after Harold's demolitions at the old Saxon burh or whether it was a complete rebuild using recovered masonry?

The castle scene here informs us the army has just left Hastings, the Norman soldier to the right representing the tail end of the army marching off to do battle. One thing is clear: the third scene is not of the prefabricated lower wooden fort.

Both *The Carmen* and William of Poitiers agree that William was fearful of losing his ships so built ramparts and ditches to protect them, as well as his men, from attack. This causes us to doubt Battle Abbey's account of the greater part of William's ships being deliberately burnt:

Figure 6.3 The caption in this image informs us the army have left Hastings represented by two towers, a connecting wall and a very solid entrance door.

> And having burnt the greater part of the ships (lest any of his followers, relying upon the hope of returning home, should be careless in the design that they had undertaken).

It is more likely that firewood was in short supply in the immediate vicinity of the landing and they burnt some boats as fuel for cooking and metal working and even to provide warmth on the cold October

ERECTING THE UPPER AND LOWER FORTS AT HASTINGS

nights. The Battle Abbey account was written a century after the Battle of Hastings and if they had heard boats were burned perhaps it caused them to exaggerate the event to enhance the heroic image of Duke William and his army, having them forego their means of escape and ensuring that they had to fight to the end if necessary – an unlikely plan.

William of Jumièges' *Chronicle* confirms that the duke erected two castles at Hastings. Nick Austin in his *Secrets of the Norman Invasion* shows these were constructed on two levels, the lower position established immediately after landing on the banks of Combe Haven and a higher-level castle at what is now Upper Wilting Farm, some three-quarters of a mile to the north-west.

Anyway, William's army having arrived at Hastings faced the urgent task of securing a foothold strong enough to withstand attack. He had his boats dragged ashore and according to Wace, 'each ship ranged by the other's side'. What use the ships were put to next, as we have seen, is confused by the different accounts.

Chapter 7

King Harold Selects his Battlefield – the Highest Hill

> 'On the highest point of the summit he planted his banner.'[1]

As we have seen, Duke William with his army arrived at Hastings on the morning of Friday, 29 September and set up defences about Redgeland Wood, or Hrycglande as it might have been known at the time.

In the meantime, while William was preparing his troops and scouting the surrounding area where he was expecting to do battle, Harold's army was resting and licking its wounds after thoroughly defeating the Norwegian army under King Harald Hardrada at Stamford Bridge four days earlier on 25 September. But it was not long before he was on the road south to confront the Norman army he had been expecting all summer, having learnt of its landing in East Sussex.

Henry of Huntingdon relates Harold's hurried departure south from Yorkshire after learning of Duke William's landing on the south coast:

> Harold, king of England, returned to York the same day, with great triumph. But while he was at dinner, a messenger arrived with the news that William, duke of Normandy, had landed on the south coast, and had built a fort at Hastings. The king hastened southwards to oppose him.

In an epic dash south, he arrived in London on Monday, 9 October and, after consolidating his forces, set out for Hastings a couple of

KING HAROLD SELECTS HIS BATTLEFIELD

days later. There is hardly any information available about Anglo-Saxon tracks and roads in eleventh-century England, but it is thanks to the work of Ivan Margery that we know the routes of the Roman road in East Sussex. Watling Street,[2] running from London to the main Channel crossing point to the continent at Dover, would have been Harold's 'rapid transit' way to the south-east. The Roman road branch from Watling Street at Rochester gives access to the bloomery in Beauport Wood and on to Hastings – the line of this branch can be traced most of the way as it passes over the hills of the Weald and through the densely wooded country that still largely remains today.

But the fact is that the army reached the site where the battle would be fought the next day, late on Friday, 13 October, or early morning the next day, the day of the battle. That the distance of nearly 60 miles was covered in just two days, speaks volumes for the quality and durability of Roman construction and no doubt Saxon road maintenance efforts as well.

We could reasonably surmise the course taken was south-eastwards from London to Tonbridge and then along the route of the present day A21. If so, then the route runs less than 2 miles north-east of our proposed battle site (the most elevated land around) just to the east of the present-day village of Telham. The OS map shows a wooded (coppiced) area lying between the A21 and the battlefield site. *The Carmen*'s description of the Saxons taking possession of the battle site states:

> There was a hill near the forest and a neighbouring valley and the ground was untilled because of its roughness. Coming on in massed order – the English custom – they seized possession of this place for the battle.

This provides the first of our clues to the location of the site of the historic Battle of Hastings. The deep neighbouring valley lies just below the (battle) hill to the east of it. The site, shown on Figure

9.2, is adjacent to the woods (now known as Beauport Park) from which the Saxons emerged after their dash from London. There is no reason to believe that the woods were not there in 1066, since the area held the third most important Roman bloomery in the empire and would have been used for harvesting wood for the charcoal that fed the furnaces to smelt the iron ore. There is no reason to believe they were not producing in the eleventh century as they were in the early nineteenth.

Arriving during the night before the battle, Harold would not have had time to prepare proper defences, yet Henry of Huntingdon's account: 'Harold had formed his whole army in close column, making a rampart which the Normans could not penetrate,' informs us that ramparts were made and that some excavation work must have been completed beforehand – perhaps they were part of permanent defences; after all, there was an iron industry thereabouts and remains of ancient habitations.

Wace says much the same thing:

> So he [King Harold] would not be detained, but set out from London, leading his men forward armed for the fight, till he reached where the Abbey is now built.[3] There he said he would defend himself against whoever should seek him; and he had the place well examined, and surrounded it by good fosse [ditch], leaving an entrance on each of three sides, which were ordered to be well guarded.

Whether these defences were pre-existing in their entirety or were hurriedly augmented before the battle we cannot know. Nevertheless, Harold needed to defend his kingdom against the Norman invasion and had chosen his defensive position well. The site meets most of the requirements for a medieval defensive position, being situated on a jutting spur of land. It has a steep slope to the west where it would make it very difficult or impossible to mount a cavalry charge; the contour-hugging defence line winding northwards at the ends is ideally suited for defence against outflanking manoeuvres. The east and west flanks of the Saxon line are close to each other, about 550yds apart in our model, so that reserves held inside the perimeter or troops moving across the perimeter could rapidly transfer to wherever they were needed. Finally, and importantly, the ground to the north of the perimeter is sloping, albeit fairly gently, uphill. So if the line came under pressure forcing a withdrawal, it would not be at a disadvantage with the enemy above pushing down-slope with gravity on its side.

The weakest point in the line is on the Saxons' left flank where the slope is less marked and would require more men and perhaps stronger earthworks to compensate.

This site is superior to the postulated traditional site at Battle Abbey. At Battle the ground is only rising by 4 per cent and for considerably less than a mile, after which the slope reverses and is downhill to the north – the Norman army's line of attack. Saxon infantry forced to retreat would soon find the cavalry above them charging forward with gravity assisting them. What also has to be considered is that cavalry faced with a significant slope would approach it obliquely instead of head-on, reducing the effective gradient. They would turn in to attack the line at the last moment, hitting the line without a loss of momentum. So for hill defences to be effective, they needed to be very steep indeed, at Battle they are not – it is inconceivable Harold chose that site to defend.

Finally, the topography at Battle does not provide natural defences against flanking attacks from either side – Blackhorse Hill does.

An alternative site mooted at Crowhurst fares little better in this respect with its 7 per cent slope. It does, however, benefit from the slope extending several miles northward, meaning a more prolonged and debilitating effort pushing the retreating foe backwards.

The Battle Abbey and Crowhurst sites, then, are comparatively flat compared with Blackhorse Hill and could not have held William's experienced and fresh troops for the nine hours or so they did. Harold, at the Blackhorse Hill site, had only to hold his line till nightfall and William's army would have been forced to return back to camp at Wilting. Meanwhile, Harold should have benefited from the arrival of a dribble of levies as the battle raged; William's time would have passed.

That this did not happen is due, according to the chronicles, to a breakdown of discipline in the Saxon army when William's tactics changed; the famous feints where his troops were ordered to feign retreat. These, no doubt largely cavalry elements, turned on the jubilant charging Saxon foot soldiers who, it seems, had fallen for the ploy and had broken out from the shield wall line on the top of the hill. Saxon soldiers were slaughtered in large numbers and the army suffered a reverse from which they were unable to recover; of which more later on.

Earlier we noted that some opinions maintain that William was preparing for a defensive battle, hence his fortifications at the old port of Hastings and Wilting. This proposition is based on William having plundered (the chronicles use the word 'wasted') the countryside for supplies but also to enrage his adversary drawing him into an ill-advised attack. But Harold was not going to leave his 'dug-in' position on Blackhorse Hill. The duke was forced to take the initiative and led his army up the rising ground and launched his army on the Saxon wall. This was at about nine in the morning of 14 October.

So what happened next?

Firstly, William's intention had been a defensive battle – a reasonable assumption – but, if correct, the strategy changed. It had to. It seems likely reconnaissance parties had seen the Saxon army occupying and strengthening a strong defensive position, meaning that William must attack if he wanted to achieve his goals. Secondly, William must have expected the Saxon army to have been diminished and weakened after Stamford Bridge and be in no position to mount an attack.

KING HAROLD SELECTS HIS BATTLEFIELD

There is the possibility that Duke William and the King of Norway had allied to better ensure victory. After all, William was of Viking stock himself and it seems conceivable they had agreed to split the kingdom between them, once Harold had been defeated. That the Norwegian king had been unexpectedly roundly beaten meant William was on his own. But waiting for Harold to attack was no longer an option and an immediate attack had to be mounted now the Saxon army was in sight on the heights above, gathering strength.

Chapter 8

The Normans March to Battle

In an earlier chapter we saw the Norman army leaving the security of the two forts they had erected on the banks of Combe Haven and the Wilting Farm area at Hastings to meet the Saxon army in the battle to decide who was to rule England. What is of interest here is the route taken to the battlefield site and the time the army might have taken to travel that route. With our knowledge from the accounts of the time, the battle commenced (9 a.m.) and through our evaluation of the terrain over which the army most likely passed, we have been able to assess whether the march to the battlefield could have been made in the daylight hours before the start of battle. But first we will look at the Norman pre-battle activities.

William of Malmesbury's account confirms the Normans remained in camp until dawn: 'the Normans passed the whole night in confessing their sins, and received the communion of the Lord's body in the morning,' ruling out a night march. It is unlikely they spent the whole night in prayers though; more probably, individual groups were doing so and then returning to their tents and quarters to rest for the deadly fight ahead.

The English, on the other hand, as William of Malmesbury has it, 'passed the night without sleep, in drinking and singing, and in the morning proceeded without delay against the enemy'.

Perhaps this was negative propaganda Malmesbury had heard. The story was unlikely, given the seriousness of the threat that faced them and that the Saxon army was so sufficiently robust on the day, it came close to defeating the Normans.

Topographical model of the greater battle of Hastings area. Note: each grid square is 1km, or 0.62 miles.

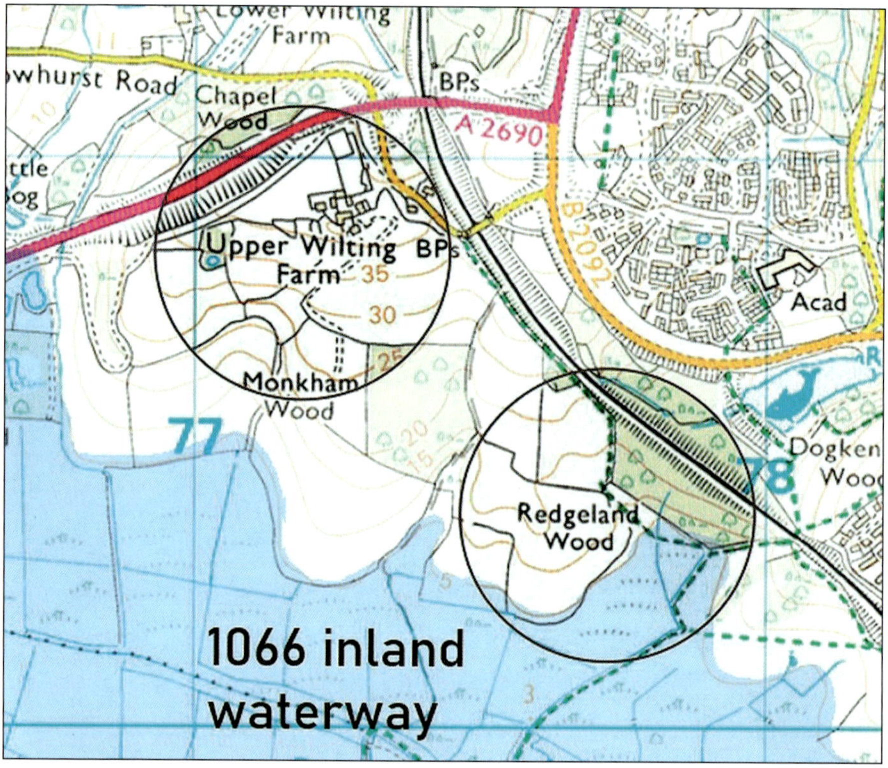

OS map (marked up) showing part of modern Hastings, and how Combe Haven as an inland waterway might have looked in 1066.

Google Earth outlines of the old Port of Hastings.

Artist's impression of the medieval port of Hastings at Combe Haven – John Tucker.

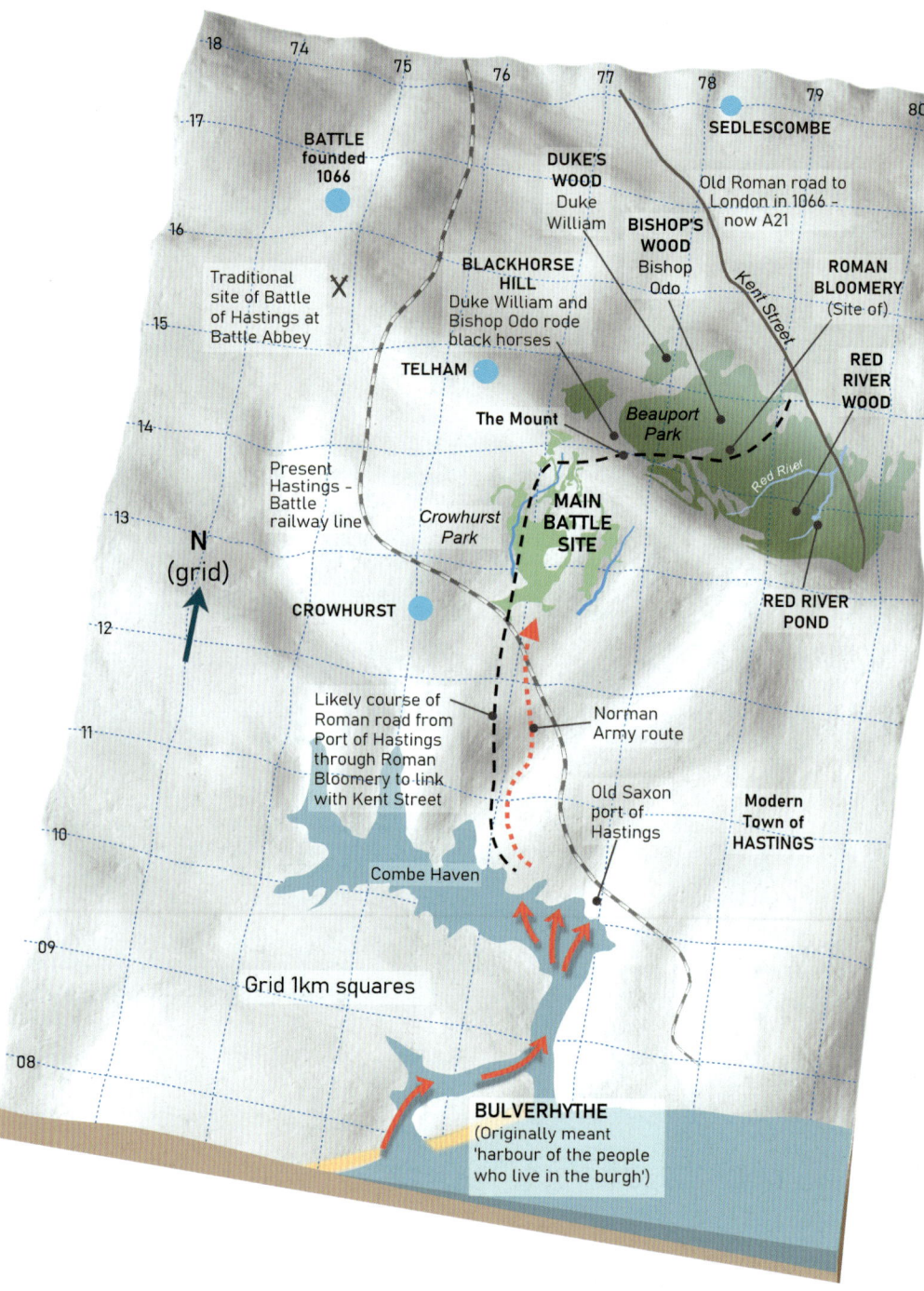

Landscaped model showing 1066 features and events in relation to present-day landmarks.

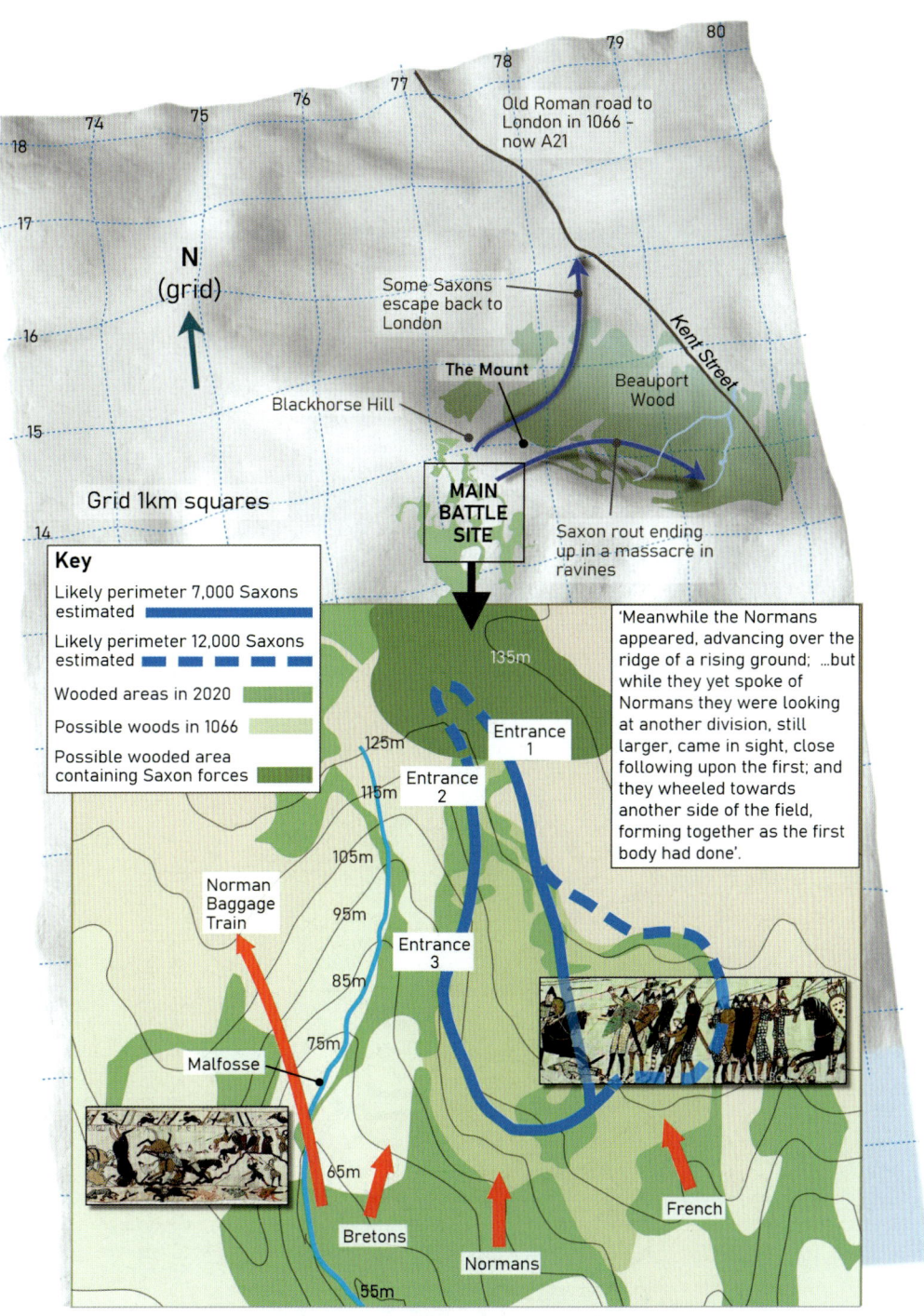

Location of Blackhorse Hill battlefield, disposition of Norman and Saxon forces at the start of the battle and their relationship to Beauport Wood.

BAYEUX TAPESTRY: HIC CECIDERUNT ANGLI FRANCI PR[O] ELIO – Here English and French fell at the same time. Circled 'principally Normans in pursuit of the English were suffocated … the pit, from this deplorable accident is still called 'Malfosse'. Note: The reed-like objects could instead be stakes intended to maim Norman calvary.

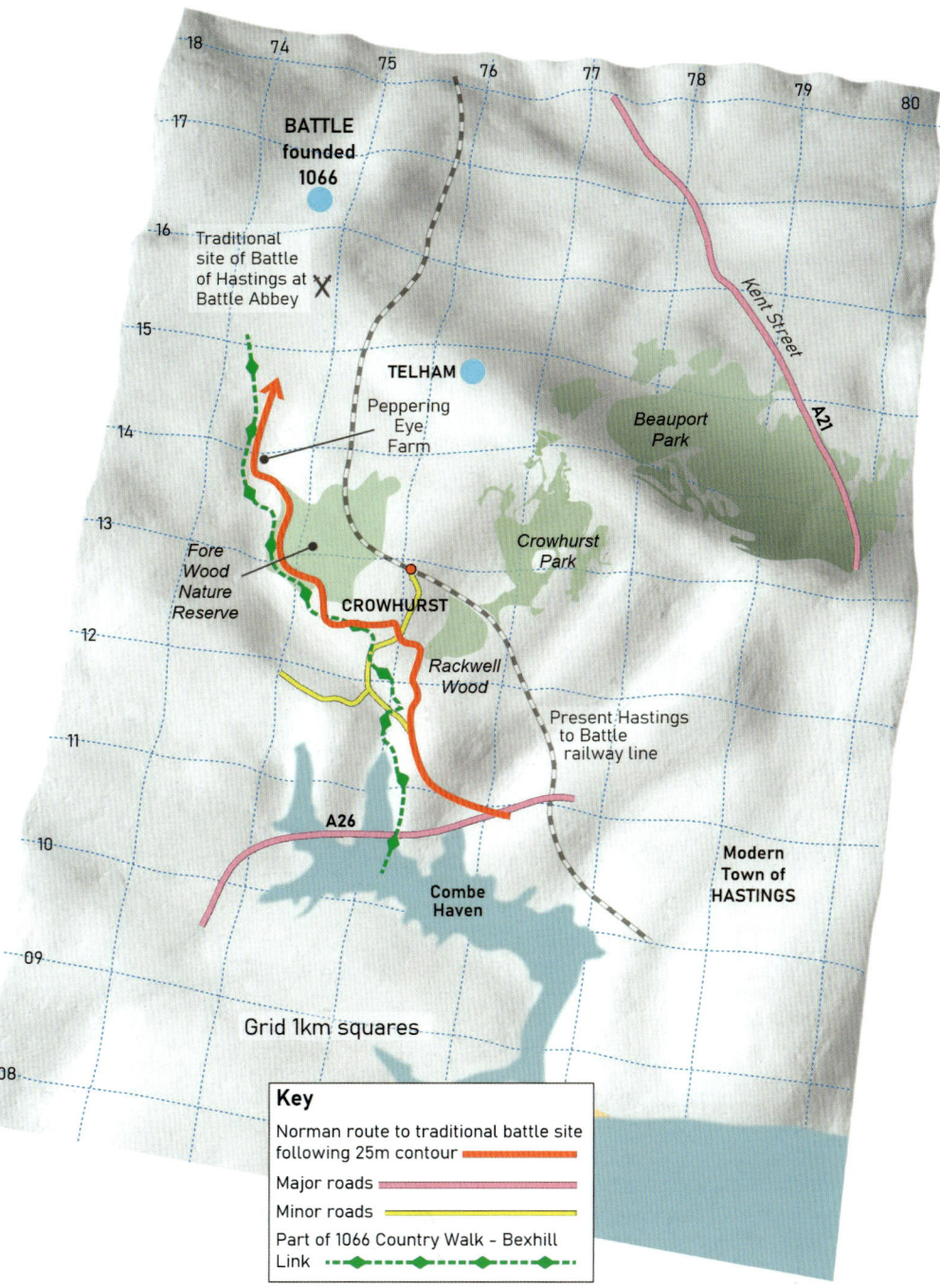

Wiltings Farm to the Battle Abbey traditional site following the 25m contour for most of the distance.

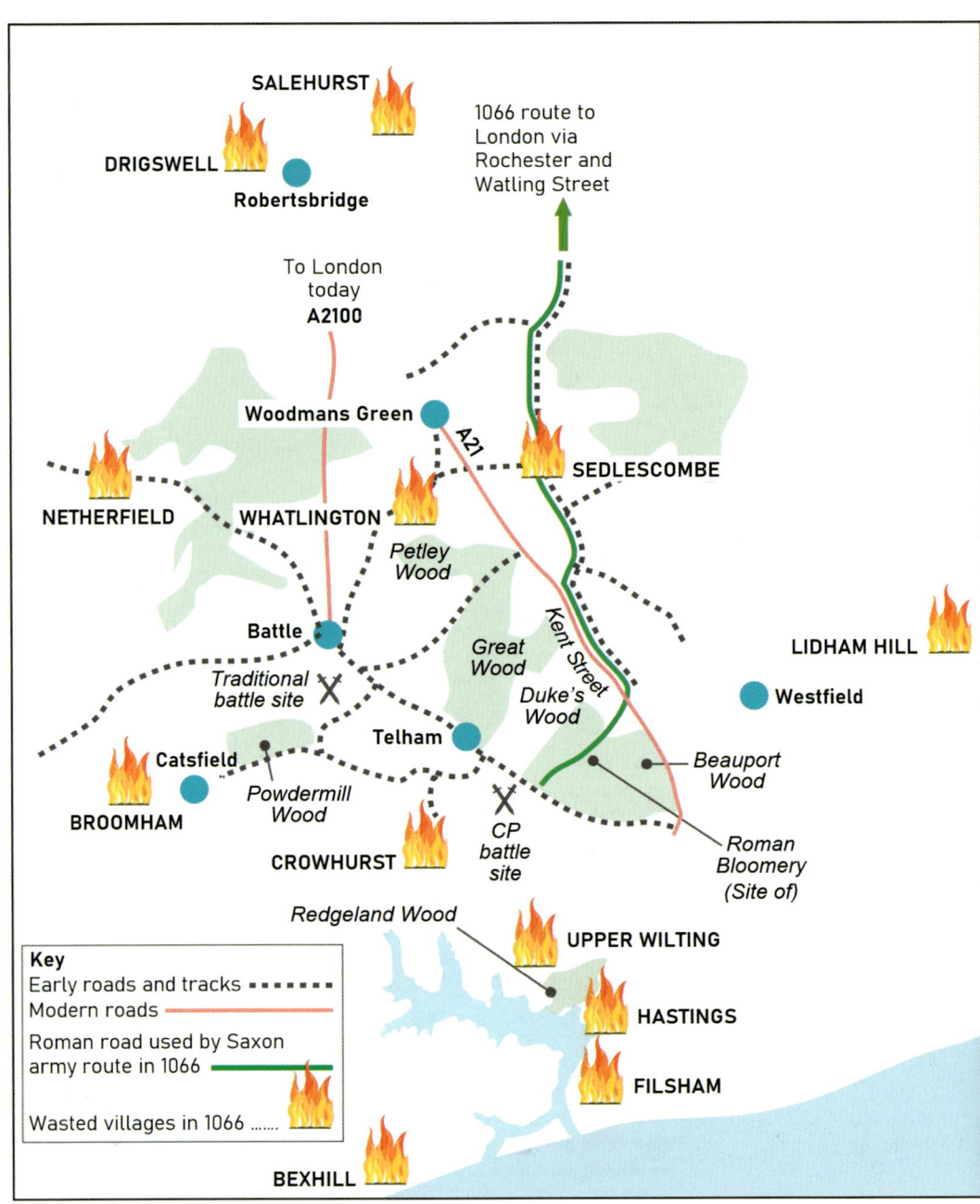

Map of East Sussex showing the area wasted by the Norman army before and after the Battle of Hastings.

Orderic Vitalis' account also has the Normans remaining in camp overnight:

> Duke William, having intelligence of Harold's approach, ordered his troops to take to their arms on the morning of Saturday. He then heard mass, strengthening both body and soul by partaking of the consecrated host.

as does Wace:

> And when the masses were sung, which were finished betimes in the morning, all the barons assembled and came to the duke, and it was arranged they should form three divisions, so as to make the attack in three places.

The Parley

An earlier chapter tells of earnest liaisons taking place between the leaders prior to battle, each hoping the other would give way and resolve the issue without the spilling of blood. This sort of thing was not uncommon before medieval battles. *The Carmen* relates that King Harold dispatched a monk to ride out to make contact with the duke. Arriving at the Norman camp, the monk passed the king's message to William, telling him: 'As matters are now, it is necessary that you leave our land. The king and the nobles command you to withdraw immediately,' meaning presumably, unhindered passage home, but, *The Carmen* adds, it was conditional on releasing prisoners captured and return of the spoils taken. A pretty uncompromising stand, but then a medieval king could do no other. Refusal, the duke was bluntly told, meant war.

Duke William's response was equally unequivocal, and predictable, dismissing the offer and the threat. But in William's initial reply, he tells the monk the idea that he should return home, is 'insanity' and the 'height of madness', because of the difficulty of the voyage so late in the season. A surprising and improbable response from a renowned hard-nosed ruler; why would the difficulty of returning home and abandoning a mission supported by the pope bother William when he had come to do battle if necessary?

Anyway, William replied, telling the monk what the king could do with his offer, saying the king had broken his pact with him: promising to support his claim to the throne on the death of Edward the Confessor; stealing the realm that should lawfully have been his. William then offered his terms: peace and a pardon provided he 'confesses his transgressions'. His lands, 'The fief his father once held',[1] restored if Harold was 'willing to be my [his] vassal now as he was formerly'.[2] Sufficiently chastened, no doubt, 'the monk hastened his journey back; [and] the duke prepared for battle'. But these exchanges seem a little unreal and maybe an embellishment added for effect.

Wace has an alternative, perhaps more likely, account of events that morning:

> At break of day in the morning, Harold rose and Gurth [his brother] with him. Noble chiefs were they both. Two warhorses were brought for them, and they issued forth from their entrenchment. They took with them no knight, varlet on foot, nor squire; and neither of them bore other arms than shield, lance and sword; their object being to reconnoitre the Normans, and know where and how they were posted. They rode on, viewing and examining the ground till from a hill where they stood they could see the Norman host, who were near, on return to camp the king sent forth two spies to reconnoitre the opposite troops, and see what barons and armed men the duke had brought with him.

The two spies fell into William's hands but were treated well,[3] and, if you believe it: 'had them taken through all the tents, and shewed the whole host to them', generously providing them with the intelligence sought.

It was akin to letting the king know they had nothing to conceal, being so confident in their superiority Harold might as well discover what he was facing. The two 'spies' were then let go and went back to inform the king of the encounter.

Historians tend to treat *The Carmen*, almost contemporary with the battle, with caution. We have to consider the monk's parley with William probably was a construct, written to court favour with the duke by establishing an enduring justification for the invasion and the blood spilt. If the monk's account is true, then the king must have dispatched the monk and spies out simultaneously for the journeys to have been completed before battle commenced. But this double dealing, negotiating whilst at the same time spying, would have been seen as dishonest and unlikely in an age where deceit of this sort would have been regarded with disdain across Europe.

In reality, Harold's reconnaissance and the length of time to complete it would have depended upon the prevailing weather conditions. On the day of the battle it did not rain, otherwise accounts would surely have mentioned it, meaning visibility that early morning was probably reasonably good. King Harold, having just arrived at his Blackhorse Hill defensive position, needed to assess the opposition; he would have been anxious to take an immediate look. His little sortie to observe the Norman camp might well have started at 6 a.m. or even earlier and he would not have had to travel very far to reach the high ground where he could get a glimpse of the opposing camp lower down the slope at Combe Haven. Harold would not have been foolish enough though to risk capture by wandering too far and we can reasonably speculate that his view of the Norman encampment soon after light, was too limited to satisfy him. So it was his desperate need for intelligence that prompted his sending the two spies.

Had the Norman Army Time Enough to Reach the Blackhorse Hill Battlefield?

The Norman army, thought by modern historians to be about 7,000 strong, and assuming a twenty-man column width, would equate to 350 ranks stretching out from van to rear. Allowing for ground conditions (woods, slope and marsh) 10ft separation between ranks including men, horses and wagons, the column would have been 5,000ft in length, or approximately a mile.

The 'as the crow flies' route from Wilting Farm to the Normans' start line at Blackhorse Hill (taken from the OS 1:25,000) is 1.6 miles, and the associated profile (Figure 8.1) is in accord with Wace's description that: 'the first division of their troops moved along the hill and across a valley.' This route profile to the start line below the Saxons' defences at Blackhorse Hill understates the actual distance. The distance along the old Roman road or other tracks used to move processed iron ore from Beauport bloomery to the port at Hastings would have meandered around hillocks and dips in the surface and been a little further. Allowing say 20 per cent additional mileage, the army would have covered some 1.92 miles.

This writer and his daughter took nearly two hours walking at a steady pace to cover the distance from Wilting Farm to Blackhorse Hill. This was a little further than the Norman army had to travel to the start line and our time included a few extra minutes' route finding. Troops clad in heavy chain mail and carrying weapons and provisions would need to pace themselves over the rising ground to arrive fresh for the fight. If they were moving at the pace of the slowest (ox carts and other supporting transport), then perhaps a reasonable speed of 2mph could be expected.

Then we have to remember, of course, that the rear would arrive sometime after the vanguard. When the van of the army reached the battle start line, the rear would still have a mile to travel (we have estimated above that the column would have been about a mile long). So for the whole army to reach the start line and moving at 2mph, it would take (1.92 + 1) ÷ 2.0 hours,[4] or 1.46 hours. Allowing additional time to form up, the army's move might take two hours altogether.

THE NORMANS MARCH TO BATTLE

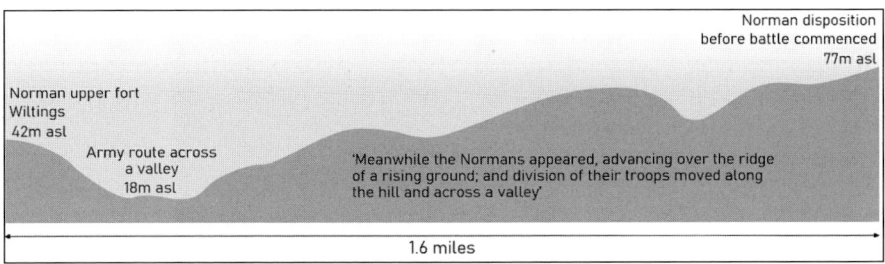

On 14 October, astronomical twilight (full darkness ends) began at 05.34, nautical twilight (first light) at 06.12 and civil twilight (dawn) at 06.50. The Battle of Hastings is recorded as having started three hours after daybreak, therefore about 9 o'clock, so the army would have had to have started out from Wilting upper fort area about 7 o'clock to be ready for battle at the said time. This means there was enough daylight for the duke's army, starting from Hastings (port area), to reach Blackhorse Hill battlefield by 9 a.m.[5]

There is also the consideration of the stories of the monk and the spies sent to the duke – if true, the duke would still have had time to deal with either or both incidents before setting out to battle. William did not need to head the column; on his sturdy steed he could have reached the battlefield comfortably in an hour, so did not have to leave Hastings before eight o'clock.

The Norman Army March Out from their Camp

Before marching off to battle, the duke delivered a rousing speech to galvanise his soldiers for the fight ahead. To boost morale, he praised the warrior qualities of his troops by contingent, *The Carmen* reporting:

> O you whom France has famed for nobility has bred, chivalrous warriors, renowned young men whom God himself chooses and whom he favours, whose lasting and unconquered name for valour resounds through the four quarters of the world.

and a warning:

> And you, race of Bretons, whose honour shines forth in arms, for whom – unless the earth itself should flee away – there is no flight.

He then, in turn, praised his French, Bretons, men from Maine, Apulia, Calabria and Sicily contingents. Reserving to last, praise for his Norman soldiers. There followed condemnation of King Harold, for his deceit and lies and adultery. And Wace records the same warning against flight in the forthcoming battle:

> You may fly to the sea, but you can fly no further, you will find neither ship nor bridge there; there will be no sailors to receive you; and the English will overtake you and kill you in your shame.

With that, the Norman army left the protection of its defences. Wace tells of Saxons seeing their approach in the distance as they 'appeared, advancing over the ridge of a rising ground; and the first division of their troops moved along the hill and across a valley' and 'as they advanced King Harold saw them afar off'.

Wace continues that King Harold watched the first troops arriving and deploying below him and:

> The youths and common herd of the camp whose business was not to join battle, but to take care of the harness and stores, moved off towards a rising ground. The priests and clerks also ascended a hill, there to offer up prayers to God, and watch the event of the battle.

and later:

> Harold saw William come, and beheld the field covered with arms, and how the Normans divided into three companies, in order to attack in three places.

THE NORMANS MARCH TO BATTLE

But could Duke William have marched his troops out of camp at Wilting before dawn and so have reached the Battle Abbey battlefield on time? Well yes in theory, even allowing for the difficulty of moving such a large force in the dark over unfamiliar wooded and boggy ground lacking proper roads or even tracks. At night, of course, they would have been exposed to ambush. But we have already seen that the Norman army stayed in camp overnight – William of Poitiers' account confirms it:

> [T]he duke ordered his men to stand by their weapons from dusk to dawn in case of a night attack.

Wace also rules out a night march telling us that King Harold and his brother Gurth rose at daybreak to reconnoitre the Norman camp:

> At break of day in the morning Harold rose and his brother Gurth with him. … They rode on, viewing and examining the ground, till from a hill where they stood they could see those of the Norman host, who were near. They saw a great many huts made of branches of trees, tents well equipped, pavilions and gonfanons; and they heard horses neighing, and beheld the glittering of armour.

The account continues, indicating that the Normans' mass finished in the morning:

> And when the masses were sung, which were finished betimes in the morning, all the barons assembled and came to the duke, and it was arranged they should form three divisions, so as to make the attack in three places.

Then: 'The duke stood on a hill, where he could best see his men; the barons surrounded him, and he spoke to them proudly … . Then all went to their tents and armed themselves as they best might.'

Clearly, if Harold and his brother saw the Normans in camp 'at break of day in the morning' and the duke 'could best see his men' then the Norman army must have left camp after daybreak and could not possibly have reached the more distant Battle Abbey battleground by nine o'clock – there was no battle at the Battle Abbey site.

That the Norman army moved slowly is borne out by William of Poitiers' account:

> Undeterred by the roughness (asperitate) of the ground, the duke with his men climbed slowly up the steep slope (*ardua cliui sensim ascendit*).

The close proximity of Blackhorse Hill to the Norman camp at Combe Haven is consistent with the in-camp activities continuing after daybreak: religious services; battle preparations; William's address to his troops; and still time to reach the start at 9 o'clock.

Further consideration of the traditional battlefield at the Battle Abbey site and the route to it is made in Appendix 3.

Chapter 9

The Battle

There are a number of contemporary written accounts of the Battle of Hastings and the lead-up to the battle that still endure today; this is quite surprising considering how few people had the facility to write and record events at the time. In spite of that, historians piecing together what transpired in 1066 from those accounts are faced with a scarcity of information that can be relied upon to help identify the location of the battlefield, the primary concern of this book.

However, buried in these historic texts are some tantalising clues: these would pass unnoticed though, if those investigating the topography are at the wrong site, the historical records describing terrain would seldom fit the lie of the land. This has been the methodology used in this book to determine the battle site in the first instance, by the application of painstaking 'trial and error', until a good match has been obtained between the actual topography and other geographical features and those few descriptions appearing in the texts.[1] The immovable 'road block' to discovery hitherto has been the unquestioning belief[2] in the traditional site at Battle Abbey. The monks compiling the *Chronicle of Battle Abbey*, the account which recalls the provenance (as they would have it) of the abbey, stated that the battle site location was unsuitable for a monastery. We believe this to be the issue that resulted in the Battle Abbey site becoming established as the site for the Battle of Hastings. The monks then allowed the abbey site to be thought as the true battlefield and as a result, memory of the actual site's location came to be lost in the mists of time. Histories of the battle, as a result, are peppered with speculation[3] as historians struggle to reconcile the discrepancies between the terrain of the supposed battlefield and descriptions in the historic texts.

The Battle Abbey account, written a century after the battle, established an entrenched belief so strong that even to contemplate alternatives has been seen as akin to an act of heresy – this argument is explored in Chapter 13. Today, satellite imaging and other recently available tools have facilitated the study of the terrain and enabled the results to be compared with the few clues appearing in the historical documents mentioning landmarks and the general battle area of October 1066.

In earlier chapters we have looked at the ground occupied by the Norman army in the days before battle commenced. It has been the discovery of the old port of Hastings on the banks of Combe Haven, and the adjacent Saxon burh earthworks that has made this possible. The port and Saxon burh together afforded Duke William a sufficiently large defensive area to accommodate the large number of men and horses and terrain suitable for defence against any surprise Saxon attack before his army was ready. We also studied the movement of the Saxon army into their defensive position on the high ground some 2 miles to the north of them.

We looked at the evidence regarding the defensive preparations made by the Saxon army for the inevitable battle and how these relate to the topography of the site identified. The seven distinct phases of the day-long battle we have identified follow on from this. On the ground, we looked for any possible signs of these preparations still enduring today. We looked at how the battle site was chosen and how these preparations benefited the Saxon army and its style of fighting to the extent that a depleted and exhausted army was able to fend off a superior force of mounted knights and archers as well as infantry for nearly nine hours of battle. If we can successfully explain this, together with the case already made for this general area for the battle, then the site of the Battle of Hastings will have been identified beyond any

THE BATTLE

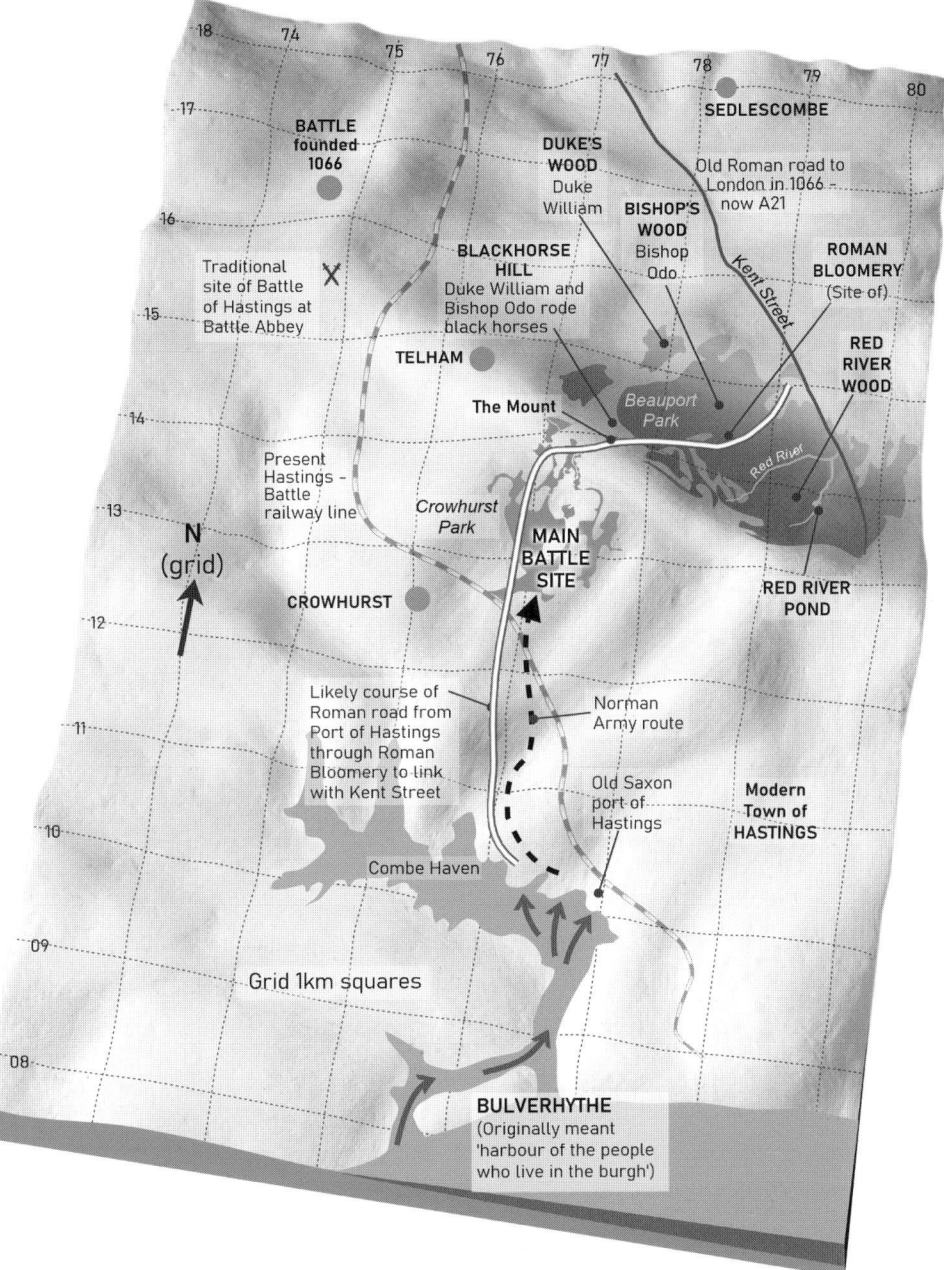

Figure 9.1 Landscaped model showing 1066 features and events in relation to present day landmarks. See colour plate section.

reasonable doubt. If this book persuades archaeologists to investigate the terrain, it could provide the supporting evidence to consolidate the case made, as well as leading to a greater understanding of the course the battle took and the reasons for the eventual Saxon defeat.

So here we reconstruct, as far as the evidence permits, the geographical extent of the battle and the Saxon defensive position by demarcating the hill site at Blackhorse Hill (the location is described in Notes to Readers). Because we do not know for certain the numbers deployed by King Harold, the battlefield map (Figure 9.2) gives two possible defensive perimeter limits based upon an army of 7,000–12,000 men.

Harold's Army Occupies the High Ground at Blackhorse Hill

The merits of the defensive position on Blackhorse Hill have already been examined in Chapter 7. Here we look at the Saxon army's occupation of the chosen defences on the night before the battle. *The Carmen*'s opening scene of the battle is, in part, described here with the arrival of the first Saxon units and their seizure of the defensive heights. The full *Carmen* account runs:

> Suddenly the forest poured forth troops of men, and from the hiding-places of the woods a host dashed forward. There was a hill [mons] near the forest and a neighbouring valley [vallis] and the ground was untilled because of its roughness. Coming on in massed order – the English custom – they seized possession of this place for the battle.

Some accounts suggest that the duke had also intended to occupy the same defences as the king, indicating a prepared position, but, if so, Harold narrowly beat him to it that morning.

Harold's seizure was cleverly planned, amassing his forward troops under the canopy of the heavily wooded Beauport Park until

THE BATTLE

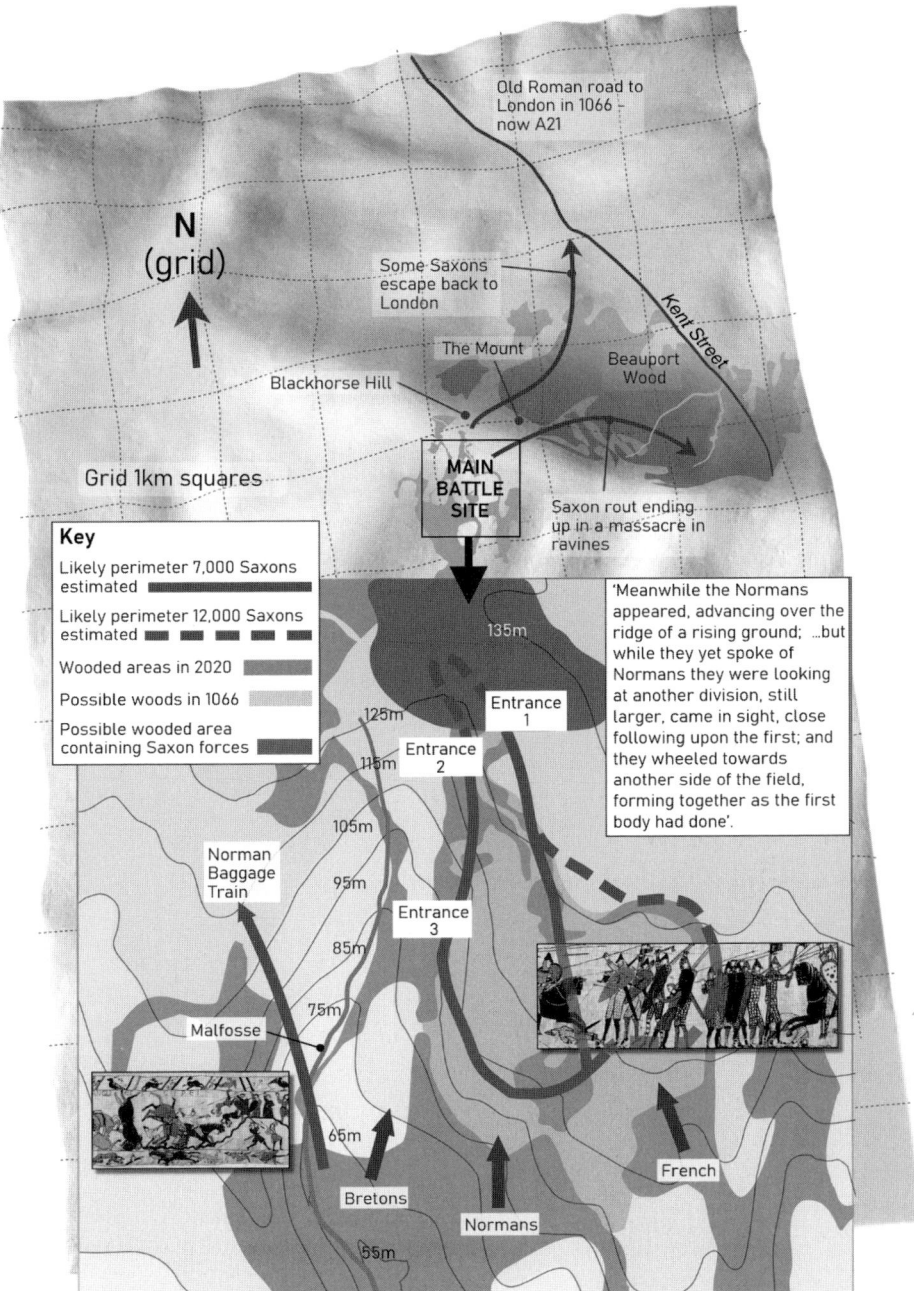

Figure 9.2 Location of Blackhorse Hill battlefield, disposition of Norman and Saxon forces at the start of the battle and their relationship to Beauport Wood. See colour plate section.

Figure 9.3 J.M.W. Turner painting from Blackhorse Hill where the Saxon defensive position was set up. The view looks southwest towards the sea and the cliffs of Beachy Head beyond Eastbourne – courtesy Tate Gallery.

there were sufficient numbers to be certain of taking the heights[4] at Blackhorse Hill. The 'hill near the forest' fits our battle site perfectly. And the neighbouring valley [vallis] shown in Figure 9.2, bounding the Blackhorse Hill site immediately to the west is also consistent with *The Carmen*'s 'vallis', the valley below being the site of the Saxons' forward defences, close by the boggy trap, the Malfosse, where many Norman knights were slaughtered that day.

William of Poitiers' account tells us much the same:

> [Harold's army] took their stand on higher ground, on a hill [montem] near to the wood through which they had come.

It seems that many troops were still arriving after the main body had taken up their positions during the night of 13/14 October and after the battle had got underway. According to Florence of Worcester's account:

> One half of his [Harold's] troops was not yet assembled, he did not hesitate to meet the enemy in Sussex, without loss of time; …. before a third of his army was in fighting order, he gave them battle.

What this passage, the king 'gave them battle' meant, is not immediately clear as it was the Normans who attacked first. Since Harold was committed to fighting a defensive battle, the phrase most likely meant he parried the first strike, meeting it with his dense shield wall – he had no alternative other than to flee. And, 'he did not hesitate to meet the enemy before his army was fully assembled', was not a choice decision; it was forced by the Normans, having already arrived in the plain below, launching their attack almost immediately. That Harold's army was able to easily withstand the Normans' opening onslaught before a third of the army was in position says much for the value of the chosen defensive position, not to mention the calibre of his army. On anything other than the steep slopes of Blackhorse Hill, Norman cavalry units would have smashed through the Saxon shield wall and destroyed the army from the rear. The battle would have been over before it had barely begun. We will argue later in this chapter that cavalry could not and was not employed in these opening stages, the slopes below the shield wall being too precipitous.

It is worth reminding ourselves here of Wace's account of the hilltop defences: 'he [Harold] had the place well examined, and surrounded it by a good fosse [ditch], leaving an entrance on each of three sides, which were ordered to be well guarded.'

Having well-guarded entrances made sense, as it allowed forays outside the shield wall to attack the Normans as opportunities arose and to swiftly retreat back inside the safety of the perimeter without disrupting the integrity of the wall. Those entrances would also have facilitated absorption of late arrivals into the defences. We are seeing here a command that knew what it was doing and also shows the chronicler understood the battle and what was important to record.

The elongated 'pear drop' shaped shield wall perimeter, narrowing to the north (solid black line or broken black line Figure 9.2), is consistent with 'an entrance on each of three sides'.[5]

Henry of Huntingdon confirms Wace's account of the earthwork defences:

> Harold had formed his whole army in close column [translator must have meant rank – see use below], making a rampart which the Normans could not penetrate.

This helps us understand the strength of Saxon defences and their role in preventing the early annihilation of the army.

Wace expounds on this, adding that:

> The English stood in close ranks, ready and eager for the fight; and they had moreover made a fosse [ditch], which went across the field, guarding one side of the army.

THE BATTLE

If the path (looking much like 'a fosse guarding one side of the army') along the western edge of Crowhurst Park today is shown to be related to the 1066 Saxon defensive works, this would be critical archaeological evidence for the site on Blackhorse Hill.

Because the Saxon army is usually depicted fighting on foot, it is assumed they did not have horses, or not in any great number. But William of Poitiers tells us that wasn't so and common sense dictates the rapid move south from Yorkshire could not have been accomplished without horses in significant numbers. They were not, however, employed as part of the main defensive formation: 'At once [the Saxons] dismounting from their horses, they lined up all on foot in a dense formation.' The tried and tested Saxon battlefield tactics of packing soldiers in tightly, leaving no gaps, made it virtually impossible for enemy infantry and cavalry to penetrate.

Orderic Vitalis' account also implies the Saxon army used horses for transport but not generally in battle:

> Dismounting from their horses, on which it was determined not to rely, they formed a solid column [should be rank] of infantry, and thus stood firm in the position they had taken.

The Carmen tells us that Harold had his wings [or flanks] strengthened with noblemen. This suggests the nobles guarding the flanks were mounted. Without horses, outside the protection of the defensive shield wall, they would have been easy pickings for the Norman cavalry.

Both William of Poitiers and Wace support Saxon defences being on a hilltop and including a surrounding ditch (there is neither sign of hilltop in the true sense of the word, nor ditch at the Battle Abbey site):

> The immense English army, here credited with Danish allies, was arrayed on a hill top. – William of Poitiers.

> Harold knew that the Normans would come and attack him hand to hand: so he had early enclosed the field in which he placed his men. – Wace

Poitier's 'hilltop' can only be one of the three southwards facing heights, spurs from the Telham escarpment described in Chapter 2, and of these, just the Blackhorse Hill 'spur' had sufficient space to accommodate an army of the size deployed by King Harold.

The way these accounts run (although it could be something lost in translation), raises the question of how the defensive ramparts could have been prepared overnight by an army arriving during the night before the battle, as popular history suggests.

Wace's story perhaps offers a clue: what was meant by Harold 'had early enclosed the field'? Are we being told that actually Harold had the defences prepared in the days, even weeks, before the battle by men remaining behind when the main army marched north to confront the Norwegians at Stamford Bridge? If so, that would explain a lot, meaning the defences were much more substantial than something prepared hastily overnight. It would also help explain how the tired and depleted Saxon army could have survived from about nine o'clock to dusk pitted against superior, fresh forces, comprising cavalry, infantry and archers – they did not spend the night digging.

There is an alternative possibility though; Colin Simmons, proprietor of the chalet complex at Crowhurst Park on Blackhorse Hill, showed this writer around the hilltop area one hot summer's day and pointed out a series of mounds and ditches in some woods nearby. Although these had not benefited from archaeological scrutiny, Mr Simmons considered these might be the remains of a medieval habitation. If so, they could have been associated with the defensive works on the hilltop, described by Wace. If Mr Simmons is right, then perhaps the 'early enclosed' could mean that Harold's army was making use of pre-existing fortifications constructed for the community's long-term defence.

THE BATTLE

There are signs of earthworks in a number of other places at and around Blackhorse Hill, but when these were constructed and for what purpose will have to await professional examination.

Saxon Troops and Weapons

The Carmen's account provides details of the Saxon army's defensive formation:

> Preparing to meet the enemy, the king … strengthened both his wings with noblemen. On the highest point of the summit he planted his banner, and ordered his other standards to be set up.

That *The Carmen* has Harold strengthening his flanks with noblemen does not contradict Wace's account, that Harold surrounded the hill with a good fosse. The steep protective slopes to the west and south sides level out on the opposite side of the perimeter that is to the south-east and north-east. Here, it would be easier for Norman cavalry to attack and smash through the defensive shield wall. Therefore, it would be no contradiction that the perimeter was strengthened by mounted noblemen positioned outside the shield wall. But there is no indication the Normans attacked in this direction.

It is fruitful to return to Wace, since his account provides the most detailed description of what were substantial Saxon defensive works and Saxon weapons:

> The English peasants carried hatchets, and keen edged bills [battleaxes, the main Saxon weapon, had long handles]. They had built up a fence before them with their shields, and with ash and other wood; and had well joined and wattled in the whole work, so as not to leave even a crevice; and thus they had a barricade in their front, through which any Norman who would attack them must first pass. Being covered in this way by their shields and barricades, their aim was to

defend themselves; and if they had remained steady for that purpose, they would not have been conquered that day.

Wace fails in this account to mention spears, an important Saxon weapon at the battle, but Baudri of Bourgeuil does:

> A rank of spears so dense that it looked like a forest and of English pressing close together in a single wedge.

Spears were a major Saxon weapon, a weapon highly effective in holding cavalry at bay, and the Bayeux battle scenes have both sides deploying spears.

Regarding the shape of the Saxon perimeter depicted in Figure 9.2, Baudri of Bourgeuil's 'single wedge' shaped boundary is consistent with it and a 7,000-strong Saxon shield wall perimeter, one of two

Figure 9.4 View looking north-west showing the valley below the shield wall defences (to the right out of the picture) on Blackhorse Hill and the slopes beyond which the Norman baggage train must have stood during the battle. When the Norman left wing started to collapse during the heat of the battle the 'varlest [bravest] who were set to guard the harness began to abandon it'.

THE BATTLE

options shown (Figure 9.2). We know from accounts that shield walls were effective, with soldiers closely packed, bunching together, with shields overlapping. The limited space available on the hill would in any case ensure that the perimeter was compact. Bourgeuil's description has been important in developing our understanding of Saxon defences on Blackhorse Hill shown in part in the photographs, Figures 9.6. and 9.7. In exposed places, like the north-east and south-east, the shield wall would have needed to be three or more rows deep.

To get an idea of how dense the perimeter line was we need a few calculations: the 7,000-troop perimeter measures some 5,000ft (1,524m), and allowing just 2ft width per man, the perimeter's front defensive line might hold some 2,500 men, leaving 4,500 men for a second or third line where the topography demanded it. Most of the eastern side of the perimeter is less steep, almost level (some 2,000ft of length) and would have needed extra rows of troops to strengthen it. This would take up, say, another 2,000 men, leaving 2,500 more held in reserve within the enclosure. They would have been tactically positioned, allowing for rapid deployment to wherever the threat was greatest.

Florence of Worcester's account (translated by Thomas Forester, 1854), graphically conveys how densely packed the Saxon army was, to the extent of being squeezed into the limited defence perimeter. It tells of the endurance of the Saxon army and that it managed to hold out from about 9 a.m. until dusk:

> The English being crowded in a confined position, many of them left their ranks, and few stood by him with resolute hearts: nevertheless he made a stout resistance from the third hour of the day [about 9 a.m.] until nightfall.

Clearly 'it was a close-run thing', to quote Wellington after the Battle of Waterloo – darkness would have ended the battle and the Norman army would have been forced to return to their camp at Combe Haven.

The account shows that Harold was finding it difficult to deploy the steady stream of troops trickling in after the battle had begun, causing some already in position to leave the field for lack of space. Perhaps the defensive perimeter established by Harold and his commanders, though initially adequate, was too small, restricting movement and delaying reinforcement of the position. The suggested defensive perimeter – shape and size, depicted in Figure 9.2 for a 7,000-man contingent, if correct, would have gained from greater flexibility to expand, but as other texts show, the fixed defences, constrained by ditches and ramparts, may have made this impossible. That is, until the ranks thinned later in the day as the battle took its toll. What we can see here is that the Blackhorse Hill hilltop made for a credible battlefield, and its topography and earthworks were consistent with contemporary accounts.

So King Harold's strategy was limited, he faced the old military conundrum: a rigid defence or mobility. But Harold could not risk a mobile battle given that his tired and weakened forces were matched against experienced, rested, Norman battle-hardened assets: squadrons of cavalry and a powerful contingent of archers; not to mention the armour-clad infantry.

The Norman army had taken up its position in the plain below Blackhorse Hill, as we have seen, at about 9 a.m. Wace describes what happened next:

> [A]ll the barons assembled and came to the duke, and it was arranged they should form three divisions, so as to make the attack in three places.

William of Poitiers takes up the story: 'the duke with his men climbed slowly up the steep slope.'

The duke, with his contingent of Normans, was positioned at the centre, climbing the steep slope.[6] The French were on the gentler slopes on the right, Figure 9.2, with Bretons occupying the left, facing an even steeper slope to that faced by the Normans and presumably

THE BATTLE

they attacked in consort with the duke and the French, although no account tells of it.

Wace, one of the most informative writers on the Normans' early movements continues:

> The youths and common herd of the camp, whose business was not to join battel, but to take care of the harness and stores, moved off towards a rising ground. The priests and clerks also ascended a hill [to the west of the battlefield], there to offer up prayers to God, and watch the event of the battel.

Wace is writing here about the Norman army's baggage train. This passage provides an important understanding of the ground they are moving to occupy: to the supposed safety of the hill rising west of the valley occupied by the Norman army and away from the Saxon defenders on Blackhorse Hill above. There is no combination of features comparable with this at the Battle Abbey battle site.

The Norman Opening Move

We have seen that Harold, since he had little alternative, had opted for a defensive battle, so the opening move was bound to be the Norman invaders', realising they would wait for ever for King Harold to attack. There are differing accounts of the opening move of the battle (phase 1), when a minstrel or juggler by the name of Taillefer begins the proceedings. Geoffrey Gaimar describes him as 'of considerable courage':

> He mounted on a fine horse – an intrepid and noble warrior. Placing himself in front of the others [the rows of troops], he performed amazing feats before the English: he seized his spear by the butt just as if it had been a little stick, threw it high into the air and caught it again by its point as it fell.

Three times he tossed the spear in this way, and by the time he raised it for the fourth time, he had come so close that he hurled it straight into the English [lines], and wounded one of the English troops as it drove into his body. He then stepped back, drew his sword, threw it high into the air and caught it again as it fell.

Taillefer's audacious suicide mission ends with the minstrel slicing off the hand of another English soldier and then being killed by spears thrown by Saxon soldiers from behind the shield wall. *The Carmen* tells it quite differently and has him 'pierce an Englishman's shield with his keen lance and hewed the head from the prostrate body with his sword', displaying 'the trophy' to his comrades. 'All rejoiced and at the same time called upon the Lord. They exulted that the first blow was theirs, both a tremor and a thrill ran through brave hearts and at once the men hastened to close shields.'

Whether or not this was a pre-planned move or Taillefer acting alone, it signalled the start of battle.

The Norman Onslaught Begins

The massed Norman divisions attacked soon after 9 a.m. *The Carmen* has archers opening the battle (phase 2) to soften up the defenders:

> First the bands of archers attacked and from a distance transfixed bodies with their shafts and the cross-bow men [balistantes] destroyed the shields as if by a hail-storm, shattered them by countless blows.

Doubt, though, has been cast on the use of cross-bows at the Battle of Hastings.[7] The effectiveness of archery at that early stage in the battle is also problematic; arrows fired from the depth of the valley below would have lost momentum as they rose to their zenith, level with the Saxon line, lacking the force to penetrate shields.

THE BATTLE

The Carmen's claim: 'shattered them [Saxon army] by countless blows', must be hyperbole, otherwise how could the Saxons have endured all day under such 'devastating weaponry'. That the Saxon king was killed or severely wounded by an arrow later in the day, if it happened (wounded by an arrow) at all, was in different circumstances, an issue addressed later in this chapter.

Wace does not mention cross-bows, but instead, describes the ineffectiveness of the archery:

> The Norman archers with their bows shot thickly upon the English; but they covered themselves with their shields, so that the arrows could not reach their bodies, nor do any mischief, how true soever was their aim, or however well they shot.

This is more realistic and Wace's description is suggestive of a loss of momentum, as alluded to above, as the missiles rose to their high point level with the Saxon army on the hill top. If the battle had taken place at the traditional site at Battle, where there is no hill high enough to cause such a loss of momentum, the damage inflicted might have been serious, even terminal.

Following the abortive archery attack, the next phase (phase 3) was the first contact. *The Carmen* tells us the French attacked the left (the Saxon left that is), the Bretons the right (the Saxon right) and the Normans, the centre. *The Carmen* continues with:

> They [the defenders] met missile with missile, sword-stroke with sword-stroke.

Bodies were piling up, but the Saxon line held and could not be penetrated; *The Carmen* continuing with:

> [B]odies could not be laid down, nor did the dead give place to living soldiers, for each corpse though lifeless stood as if unharmed and held its post.

It was a deadly battle of attrition, with Harold steadily losing men as the battle proceeded; he would have needed reinforcements to continue resisting. However, as we have seen, Harold was forced to meet the Norman opening moves before half his army had arrived. One can suppose the other half were assembling at Sedlescombe,[8] as they arrived from London, before marching forward in organised units under cover of the woods and then entering the battlefield perimeter through one of the three 'entrances'. No doubt it was the steady flow of late arrivals that saved the Saxons from being overwhelmed and an early defeat, and able to hold out until late that day.

Wace tells us the duke could not prevail against a robust Saxon showing:

> The Normans saw that the English defended themselves well, and were so strong in their position that they could do little against them.

Apart from Gaimar's Taillefer account, there are no written accounts of cavalry attacks on the shield wall whilst it still held, although the Bayeux Tapestry (Figure 9.10) shows it. It may not be a true representation of events, or alternatively, it may be showing cavalry attacking the eastern side of the perimeter where the ground was easier.

It is to be noted that unlike most medieval battles where cavalry was deployed in the early stages, the formidable Norman cavalry was not used to any significant extent at Hastings until later in the day. The slopes up to the Saxon lines (excepting on the eastern flank, which seems to have been left alone, at least in the opening stages)[9] were just too precipitous. Riders foolish enough to try, would, on reaching the defenders atop the ramparts protected by fences of 'ash and other wood,'[10] and wattle, be cut down by blows from battleaxes (bills). Riders hanging back in the saddle as they reached the top of the slope would have found it difficult to properly use their weapons and meet blow with blow; they would have fallen easy prey to Saxon soldiers above them. Together with their horses they were struck down, as told by Wace:

> He [a Saxon defender] rushed straight upon a Norman who was armed and riding on a warhorse, and tried with his hatchet[11] of steel to cleave his helmet; but the blow miscarried, and the sharp blade glanced down before the saddle bow, driving through the horse's neck down to the ground, so that both horse and master fell together to earth.

Duke William knew it was futile to attack the line whilst it was holding firm and was, no doubt, by then desperately searching for a strategy to turn the tide of battle in his favour.

So it is quite late in his account that Wace gets to the final demise of the king. But before then, it seems, the invading army met with a severe setback that nearly resulted in their defeat.

Disaster for The Duke at The Malfosse

Whether this Norman setback occurred before or after Harold was struck by an arrow, or at what point in the day-long battle it took place, is not clear. But the disaster may have been the event that precipitated or coincided with the collapse of the Breton left wing. The fight at the Malfosse (phase 4), according to Wace, was of such a scale and intensity that it almost cost William the battle:

> In the plain was a fosse, which the Normans had now behind them, having passed it in fight without regarding it. But the English charged and drove the Normans before them till they made them fall back upon the fosse, overthrowing into it horses and men. Many were to be seen falling therein, rolling one over the other with their faces to the earth, and unable to rise.

William of Poitiers distinguishes, perhaps Wace also meant to do so, between the fosse which guarded the English camp, and the ravines into which the Normans fell in pursuit during the rout – see the following chapter.

Some of the attacking English troops did not avoid becoming casualties though. Wace recounts:

> Many of the English also, whom the Normans drew along with them, died there. At no time during the day's battle did so many Normans die, as perished in that fosse. So those said who saw the dead.

Henry of Huntingdon, although somewhat ambiguous in his portrayal of the event, does seem to be describing the same episode:

> In their flight they happened unawares on a deep trench, which was treacherously covered, into which numbers fell and perished. While the English were engaged in pursuit, the main body of the Normans broke the centre of the enemy's line, which being perceived by those in pursuit over the concealed trench, when they were consequently recalled most of them fell there.

But he is also tying the event to the feint ordered by the duke, where large numbers of Saxons lost their lives making this account somewhat ambiguous.

William of Malmesbury's account, one of the most even-handed, is worth reading too, as it implies that the fosse was more than a natural feature at the foot of Blackhorse Hill on its western slope, but concealed a 'purpose made trap' where, perhaps, Harold came closest to defeating the invader and keeping his crown:

> [T]hey [the Saxons] met an honourable death in avenging their enemy; nor indeed were they at all without their own revenge, for, by frequently making a stand, they slaughtered their pursuers in heaps. Getting possession of an eminence,

THE BATTLE

they drove back the Normans, who in the heat of pursuit were struggling up the slope, into the valley beneath, where, by hurling their javelins and rolling down stones on them as they stood below, the English easily destroyed them to a man.

William of Malmesbury's continuation of the previous passage confirms the event:

Besides[,] by a short passage with which they were acquainted, they [the Saxons] avoided a deep ditch and trod underfoot such a multitude of their enemies in that place that the heaps of bodies made the hollow level with the plain.

The incident is graphically illustrated in the Bayeux Tapestry image (Figure 9.5). The reed-like objects protruding from the water below the letters '*SIMLI ANGLI*', may instead be, some speculate, sharpened stakes.

The Normans were forced to retreat in the face of the strong Saxon onslaught and we can see in this scene, horses and riders tumbling headlong into the watercourse and surrounding marshy area, unaware of its having been 'treacherously concealed'.[12]

Figure 9.5 BAYEUX TAPESTRY: *HIC CEDIDERUNT ANGLI FRANCI PR[O] ELIO* – Here English and French fell at the same time.
 Circled 'principally Normans in pursuit of the English were suffocated … the pit, from this deplorable accident is still called 'Malfosse'. Note: The reed-like objects could instead be stakes intended to maim Norman calvary. See colour plate section.

It is clear that Saxon troops were fighting outside the protection of the shield wall. *The Carmen*'s referral below, to a 'neighbouring valley', may be an indication of Saxon 'forward' forces stationed in that valley[13] in the vicinity of the fosse:

> There was a hill near the forest [from which the Saxons had just emerged] and a neighbouring valley. … Coming on in massed order, the English custom, they seized possession of this place for the battle.

But what was meant depends on whether *The Carmen*'s 'this place' was intended to include the neighbouring valley.

Harold's strategy makes good sense, his objective was simply to survive the day, that is until nightfall (around 7 p.m. on 14 October) by wearing down William's forces, while all the time receiving reinforcements from around the country. The deployment of an advanced contingent in the valley below would have additionally strengthened the Saxons' right flank picket,[14] and assisted in buying vital time by delaying Duke William's attack on the main force on the steep hill above.

If Harold could succeed in that, then any prospects of William continuing the battle another day would be out of the question without reinforcement of his depleted force and resupply from across the Channel. Failure on the 14th would have left the Norman army at serious risk of being stranded[15] and annihilation.

Figure 9.6, taken from the foot of the narrow valley to the west of and below where the Saxon shield wall line stood, fails to reveal the treacherous nature of the water-logged hollow fed from the spring higher up the valley. The bracken and thorn bushes hide what battle evidence may still lie within. It was a welcome surprise to discover this feature, one that looks very much like the site of the Malfosse even after all those centuries. Approaching as close to the edge as he dare, this writer had the sense of some long-ago catastrophe. In 1066, as graphically shown in the tapestry scene and described here in the *Chronicle of Battle Abbey*, it might have been more deadly and terrifying:

THE BATTLE

There lay between the hostile armies a certain dreadful precipice, caused either by a natural chasm of the earth, or some convulsion of the elements. It was of considerable extent, and being overgrown with bushes or brambles was not very easily seen, and great number of men – principally Normans in pursuit of the English – were suffocated in it. For ignorant of the danger, as they were running in disorderly manner, they fell into the chasm and were fearfully dashed to pieces and slain. And the pit, from this deplorable accident is still called Malfosse.

Figure 9.6 View of bramble covered swampy hollow below heights where the Saxon shield wall would have stood.

The monks of Battle Abbey describing this skirmish must have been fully aware of its location. That they failed to record it for posterity is, in itself, telling, for to have done so would have undermined their story that Battle Abbey was constructed on the actual battlefield site.[16]

This incident, one of the key events in the battle, was a set-up that the Normans fell for, showing Harold to be the able general he was by incorporating the fosse into his defensive plan. Perhaps he was not of the calibre of Duke William,

Figure 9.7 View of the high ground of Blackhorse Hill to the east – the site of the Saxon army position. The stubble field in the foreground is, according to the historical topographical description, the probable location of the Norman baggage train.

1066: THE LOST HASTINGS BATTLEFIELD

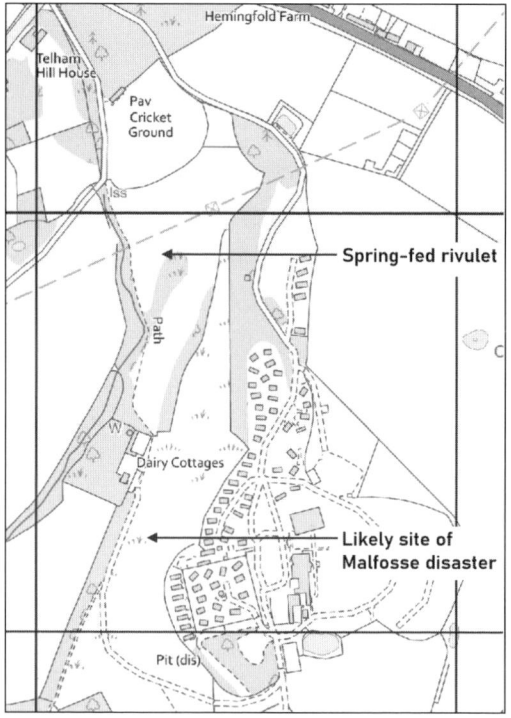

Figure 9.8 OS 1:10,000 map showing the location of the Malfosse and rivulet feeding it.

but capable of planning and executing a robust defence even when faced by superior odds. That he chose his ground wisely and used it to maximum advantage, though ultimately defeated, is demonstrated by this near triumph over the Conqueror.

It is a different image of Harold taught at school. But what is important for our story is that the battlefield terrain shown here matches historic accounts. In particular, the dramatic tapestry scene in Figure 9.5, depicting Saxon soldiers on the hillock to the right of the Malfosse, 'hurling their javelins and rolling down stones on them as they stood below, the English easily destroyed them to a man',[17] is consistent with our location for the battle.

Perhaps the tapestry exaggerates, possibly done to show the Normans in a favourable light – especially if they thought the obstacle had been 'treacherously' hidden from view. But no doubt, over the course of 1,000 years since the battle, the fosse has silted and dried, and is now less noticeable.

This skirmish, if it can be described as such, was summed up by Orderic Vitalis:

> At length the indomitable bravery of the English threw the Bretons, both horse and foot, and the other auxiliary troops

THE BATTLE

composing the left wing into confusion, and, in their rout, they drew with them almost all the rest of the duke's army, who, in their panic, believed that he was slain.

William of Poitiers had the same impression of this part of the battle, but disposed of it in just a few words: 'but after a period of fierce fighting, his [Duke William's] left wing started to collapse, causing the entire line to falter.'

According to Wace, the collapse of the Normans was almost universal, causing even the baggage train, deployed up the slope above the valley, to make a hasty retreat:

> The varlest [bravest] who were set to guard the harness began to abandon it, as they saw loss of the Frenchmen, when thrown back upon the fosse without power to recover themselves. Being greatly alarmed at seeing the difficulty in restoring order, they began to quit the harness, and sought around, not knowing where to find shelter.

Figure 9.9 *HIC EST WILLEL[MUS] DUX* – Here is Duke William.

The day was saved for the Normans by William's outstanding generalship at this critical juncture in the battle, rallying his forces by revealing that he had not been slain, the rumour spreading among his troops. The Bayeux Tapestry image Figure 9.9, shows the duke on his black horse raising his visor to reveal his face to those around him. To his right, Eustace, his colour bearer, is calling out to the demoralised troops that Duke William lives and is still commanding.

The high point for the Saxons had passed, and a series of Norman feints (phase 5 of the battle) resulted in the weakening of the Saxon army as it broke ranks and exposed itself to the Norman cavalry that had at last come into its own. The indiscipline, if that was what it was, was fatal. It was the beginning of the Saxon defeat, the army falling back from its previously secure position:

'The Englsh [*sic*] fell back upon rising ground.'[18]

The phrase: 'rising ground' is significant, the rising ground corresponds to the sloping terrain to the north of Blackhorse Hill, behind the Saxons' defensive perimeter. It rises from 100m at the shield wall's southern front, to 140m at the summit of Telham Ridge by 'The Mount' (see Chapter 11). This was another advantage of the terrain chosen by Harold and his commanders facilitating the Saxons' fighting withdrawal, the 'orderly retreat' according to Wace.

The End for Saxon England (Phase 6)

Figure 9.10 *HIC CECIDERUNT LEWINE Et GYRD FRATRES HAROLD REGIS* Here fell Leofwine and Gyrth, brothers of King Harold.

THE BATTLE

Earlier we saw Harold struck by an arrow above an eye, yet gallantly remaining in the field leading his Saxons; at least that was Wace's version of events. There are other accounts of course, including one which has been largely dismissed, with Harold killed in the early stages of the battle. This writer favours Wace's version, because Wace was writing about a century after the battle and ought, with the passage of time, to have been more impartial than contemporary accounts like *The Carmen*. Wace's account was based, he tells us, on an eyewitness description of the battle:

> I have seen many men who saw it, men of full age at the time, and who lived many years after.

and therefore carried authority.

Turning to Harold's death, Wace's description of the tragic end of the king is in agreement with most accounts: near the end of the day:

> And now the Normans had pressed so far, that at last they reached the standard. There Harold had remained, defending himself to the utmost; but he was sorely wounded in his eye by the arrow, and suffered grievous pain from the blow.

Figure 9.11 The wounding and death of King Harold.

> An armed man came in the throng of the battle, and struck him on the ventaille [in this context an attached metal strip over the nose to protect the face] of his helmet, and beat him to the ground; and as he sought to recover himself, a knight beat him down again, striking him on the thick of his thigh, down to the bone.

1066: THE LOST HASTINGS BATTLEFIELD

Wace then tells how the duke himself entered the fray, striking Harold with 'great force'. Wace is unsure whether that particular blow killed him, but Harold rose no more. *The Carmen* confirms this and being more specific, has the duke, Eustace of Pontieu, Giffard and others attacking and killing the king, though we cannot be sure that Wace is not taking his account from *The Carmen*. The Bayeux Tapestry scene Figure 9.11, displays the same story: an eye wound and a sword strike cutting into Harold's thigh, although of course the two events were separated by an unknown time lapse. After that, Wace says the Saxon army fought on until:

> The English were in great trouble at having lost their king, and at the duke's having conquered and beat down the

Figure 9.12 *ET FUGA VERTERUNT ANGLI* – and the English fled.

This grisly scene shows the remnants of the Saxon army fleeing for their lives. It's interesting to see some of the fleeing soldiers mounted, whereas horses were not used by the Saxons in the battle itself, the army: 'at once dismounting from their horse' [William of Poitiers], excepting perhaps in protecting the army's flanks. We can speculate that the symbolic tree represents the woodlands through which the chase took place.

standard; but they still fought on, and defended themselves long, and in fact till the day drew to a close.

The Carmen has much the same story, excepting claiming that the 'English refused battle' after Harold's death. Wace contradicts the assertion, saying the Saxon army fought on until 'the day drew to a close … and the news had spread throughout the army that Harold, for certain, was dead; and all saw that there was no longer any hope, so they left the field, and those fled who could.'

It seems unlikely though that the defeated Saxons would not have continued to fight, at least to defend themselves in retreat. The next chapter describes the stand made by the remnants of the Saxon army as they fled through Beauport Wood through which they had come that previous night.

Chapter 10

Rout

As long as King Harold remained alive, the Saxon resolve was maintained and the army was unbeatable, at least in the short term. The system of command and control exercised at the battle by Harold is unknown, but like the strategy and tactics adopted, it would have drawn on the experience gained over the centuries. These were clearly effective in that the army endured for so long that day. But the loss of direction and coordination with Harold's death, and the death of his two brothers, was decisive – that the king had continued commanding after suffering the severe and painful head wound, speaks volumes for his courage and endurance.

In the preceding chapter we saw the Saxon army's defeat occurred as dusk fell when Harold was killed. The English army, depleted, weakened and demoralised was overwhelmed and fled the field, pursued by Normans bent on vengeance. Some were able to melt into the forest through which they had come the night before and get back to London. Others, not so lucky, were struck down by the Norman cavalry as they fled. The pursuit continued all night and perhaps into the next day.

Wace, an important source for this final phase of the battle, recounts the experience of those fleeing the Normans' wrath:

> The English who escaped from the field did not stop till they reached London, for they were in great fear, and cried out that the Normans followed close after them. Whilst at a gully in the woods, … The press was [so] great to cross the

bridge, and the river beneath it was deep; so that the bridge broke under the throng, and many fell into the water.

But according to Orderic Vitalis the pursuit did not go entirely their way for the Normans:

> The Normans, finding the English completely routed, pursued them vigorously all Sunday night [was Saturday night intended here?], but not without suffering a great loss.

Orderic Vitalis continues describing the tragic outcome of their rashness:

> galloping onward in hot pursuit [they] fell unawares, horses and armour, into an ancient trench,[1] overgrown and concealed by rank grass,[2] and horses rolling over each other, were crushed and smothered. ... this accident restored confidence to the routed English, for, perceiving the advantage given them by the mouldering rampart and a succession of ditches (see profile Figure 10.2), they rallied in a body, and, making a sudden stand, caused the Normans severe loss.

It is not surprising that horses and riders suffered heavy losses in their uncontrolled chase through what is now Beauport Park. The park, forested land, today covering an extent of about one square mile of undulating terrain, is riven by steep-sided gullies (Figures 10.1, 10.2, 10.3 and 10.4), 15 or more feet deep; cut by the fast-running streams draining the area northwards into the Brede levels and the sea. Beneath the tree canopy, it is today largely overgrown with brambles and thorn bush; terrain difficult to penetrate on foot. If it was the same in 1066, then cavalry chasing through the twilight or night would have been heading for trouble, but no doubt their blood was up, adrenalin flowing – nothing was stopping them.

Figure 10.1 One of six ravines across Beauport Park running north-south through which the rout most probably occurred.

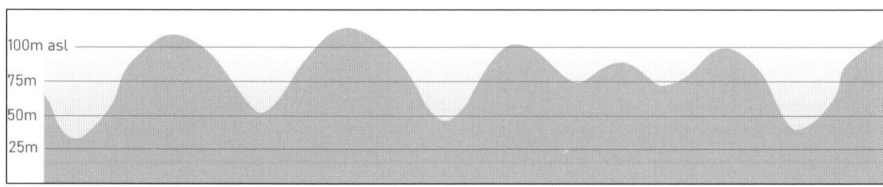

Figure 10.2 (above) Profile across Beauport Park showing treacherous obstacles to Normans and Saxons alike.

The extent of Saxon resistance that night in the woods, even though the army had been deprived of their king's leadership, suggests Duke William might still have faced a difficult fight, or series of fights, before he could regroup at his base camps at Combe Haven. But the demoralisation and terror induced by William's ruthless pursuit of the Saxons after defeat on Blackhorse Hill meant that, in the end, this did not happen.

Right: Figure 10.3 View from the foot of ravine in figure 10.1.

Below: Figure 10.4 Gully in Beauport Park wood showing steepness of sides.

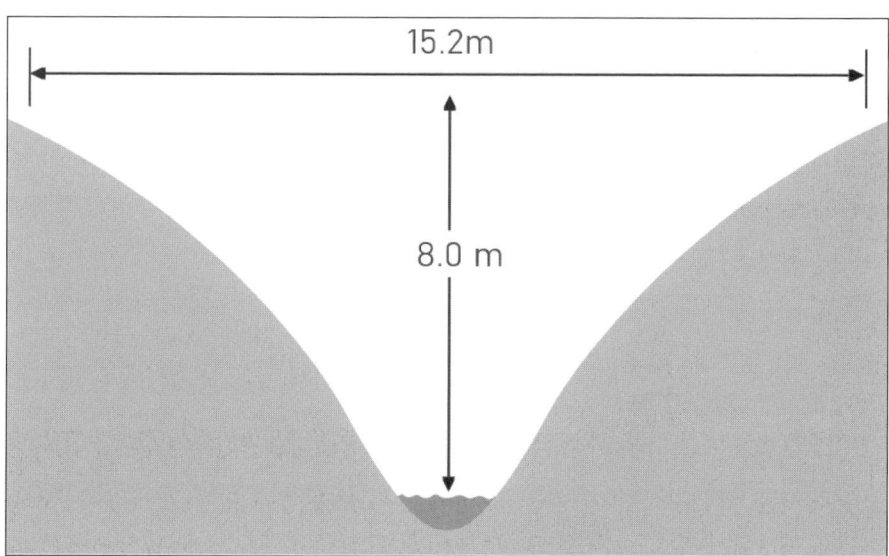

How different it might have been had these survivors later merged with troops who were unable to reach the battle in time, to organise a resistance and meet the Normans inland far from their base at Hastings. One cannot help speculating on the course of events if that unlucky (for the king and the Saxons) arrow had missed and the leadership had remained intact.

There is no indication of the number of Saxon soldiers surviving the battle after Harold's death, but it must have been significant, since up until then – while the king still commanded – they were clearly holding out against Norman pressure, even after their lines had been penetrated.

Hanging on beyond dusk into the night meant an uncertain outcome. Unless William could speedily reinforce his army, his best course would have been to sail back to France. If instead, the duke chanced his hand taking his depleted army inland, he would likely have been defeated, not by another set-piece battle, but by Saxon guerrilla tactics, disease and starvation.

After the battle, the Norman army returned to its stronghold at Hastings where it remained licking its wounds for the next two weeks. It then set out, no doubt reinforced, to take the country.

Harold's Planning

We saw in the preceding chapter in Wace's account, that Harold had 'early enclosed' the field of battle, meaning by 'early' that the defences may have been prepared long in advance or even have been permanent – a sort of hill-top village defence against raiders, such as the Vikings. The English army arrived during the night before the battle had time to beef-up defences, but not to construct anything new. Pre-constructed defences explain, at least in part, a depleted and weakened English army's ability to hold out all day against fresh Normans and other troops.

ROUT

The king's choice of battlefield and its seizure before the Normans could do so, showed Harold and his commanders were experienced and able generals. That many Saxons were able to escape the defeat on Blackhorse Hill, and still give battle in the woods and gullies behind the battlefield and some make it back to London, speaks of comprehensive pre-battle planning.

Harold may have anticipated defeat, having had first-hand experience of the fighting qualities of the duke's men two years earlier when he visited Normandy on a diplomatic mission. He would probably have known he had to find topography that gave his army a good chance of escaping a lost battle so as to, hopefully, fight another day. Behind the static defensive perimeter, to the north, lay rising ground enabling a fighting retreat. Beyond the slopes lay dense woodland[3] providing cover from pursuing Normans. The terrain there, as we have seen, was undulating, riven with gullies and generally sloping downwards in the direction back to London. It was ideal for fleeing troops, but the gullies and brambles were unhelpful to the Norman cavalry. Maybe troop leaders had been briefed on routes out to Kent Street and London. The army's dash south from Stamford Bridge was aided by horse transport not generally used in the battle. Horses held well enough back from the main battle would have assisted escape.

Our story of the rout here, constructed from the correspondence of the terrain to historical accounts, provides continuing and powerful evidence for the location of the main battlefield at Blackhorse Hill. What seem to be 'memorials' to the battle, in Beauport Park, with features carrying names of Norman commanders, imply that this phase may have been as important for the Normans as the set-piece battle before Harold's death – they needed to reduce the Saxon army to impotence before they could move on.[4]

If the scale portrayed of this encounter is correct, then it, along with the main battle on Blackhorse Hill, ought to receive recognition, as the 'Battle of Beauport Wood'. It is surprising that, although the battle was far in the distant past, there is no national memorial to the bravery shown in defence of the last Saxon kingdom. William the Conqueror would not have entertained such an idea, but because it was long in the past and the subjugated Saxon descendants have survived against the odds, that is the reason to remember.

Chapter 11

The Mount

Figure 11.1 The Mount – a mound of unknown provenance along the A2100 road adjacent to Blackhorse Hill, Beauport Wood and the bloomery. *(Credit Colin Simmons)*

Located beside the A2100 road, next to a water tower and lying in the middle of the greater battlefield,[1] lies a mound almost the height of a two-storey house and, at its base, more than a cricket pitch's length. It is not that apparent and was completely missed by this writer on the first visit to the area, even on foot, the tree coverage of

The Mount almost disguising its prominence. This mound is marked on the current 1:25,000 OS map,[2] but not named.[3] However, on the 1888–1913, 6-inch OS map, it is marked and named as 'The Mount'. It can also be seen on an old estate map dated 1744 (Figure 11.2).

It is clearly man-made; the mystery is to what end – no one seems to know.[4] Neither could anyone say whether the mound has ever been excavated by archaeologists. Here are some possibilities:

- Prehistoric burial mound
- Base for a signal beacon
- Associated with the Battle of Hastings

The mound's history, such as it is, is that during the Napoleonic Wars it served as a base for a signal beacon to foretell of the approach of any French invasion fleet and may have been used for the same purpose earlier, in the Elizabethan age, when the country was threatened by the Spanish Armada in 1588. Its elevated position overlooking the Channel and inland to form part of the network of signal beacon stations was ideal.

But what interests us here is the last-named possibility, its association with the epic battle of 1066. We turn to William Arthur MA, Etymologist. In his *Etymological Dictionary of Family and Christian Names* published in 1857,[5] there is a tantalising entry under the family name 'Mountjoy':

> This name is still retained in a division of the hundred of Battel, not far from the remains of a majestic pile reared by William the Conqueror.

Arthur then goes on to quote someone named 'Boyer'. Who was Boyer? In the records, there is an entry on the eighteenth-century writer, Abel Boyer; this Boyer was a prolific writer[6] on historical subjects in general and military subjects in particular. It is almost certain Arthur was referring to Abel Boyer (1667–1729). He was born

THE MOUNT

in Languedoc, Southern France, and moved to live in England in 1692, following religious disturbances in his country. In the second part of the Mountjoy entry, Boyer is attributed with defining '*Montjoie*': 'as a heap of stones made by a French army, as a monument to victory'.

How tantalising is that? We have a mound, a substantial feature, called 'The Mount' on some maps, right in the midst of the 1066 battlefield; we have a family name Mountjoy (in its modern rendering); we have an etymologist, Arthur, associating Mountjoy with The Mount ('the remains of a majestic pile'); and 'a heap of stones made by the French army'.

This is not a scientific connection between the prominent feature and the great battle, but the question: could The Mount, beside the A2100 road, be an ancient monument to the Norman victory? Well yes, with the feature lying in the midst of the battlefield, the probability must be high; but what did Arthur mean by 'a majestic pile'? There is ambiguity here. Did Arthur mean The Mount was a majestic pile or did he mean Battle Abbey, the site lying 2 miles away to the west in the town of Battle, was the majestic pile?

But in answer to that we must understand that Battle Abbey no longer existed at the time Arthur was writing, it having been demolished (apart from the monks' refectory) some two centuries earlier, virtually ruling out this option. Arthur would more likely have intended The Mount by the road now designated the A2100. Furthermore, the mound having appeared on a number of earlier maps as 'The Mount', it does not stretch the imagination too far to recognise that 'The Mount' is a shortened adaptation of 'Montjoy' or its French equivalent, *Montjoie*.

If The Mount is a monument to William the Conqueror's 1066 victory and also contains corpses from the battle (see Chapter 12), then this is vital evidence for the case for the 1066 battlefield on Blackhorse Hill.

Today, traffic speeds past The Mount and it, being cloaked in trees, goes largely disregarded. In the past this was not so; as long as memories held of the great battle, it might have been viewed as a place of congregation, a place to reflect. It was also a junction of roadways: the road linking the town of Hastings with the post-1066 town of Battle and on westwards, and the north/south Roman road between the bloomery to the coast, perhaps at Bulverhythe (refer to Figure 2.15, Chapter 2). Although surface signs of the Roman road are not always visible, the photograph (Figure 2.14) across from the A2100 road by The Mount, just to its north, is one of several exceptions marking out the route.

This road, by The Mount location[7] we can speculate, could have facilitated the removal of bodies from the battlefield to The Mount for burial, thereby determining its siting.

The proximity of this Roman road to The Mount is compelling evidence underpinning the case for The Mount's location being on the Battle of Hastings site. The Mount is a significant landmark in itself, it being at the very summit of the Telham Ridge, where 'on the highest point of the summit he [King Harold] planted his banner' (see Chapter 7).

There seems to be sufficient circumstantial evidence then to warrant an archaeological investigation to determine whether the mound has prehistoric origins as a burial tumulus, is connected with the Battle of Hastings, or something else. It should reveal whether Norman battle dead have been interred there – no battle remains have ever been found, although it is unlikely professional searches have been carried out on, or near, Blackhorse Hill.

One final issue remains, and that is the dropping of the name, The Mount, prominent on earlier maps, but no longer printed on modern maps. Did this loss coincide with the passing from memory of the events that took place high up on Telham Ridge nearly a thousand years ago, or was there some other reason why cartographers ceased to record it?

In the following chapter we look specifically at the burial of the dead after the battle, because battle remains, if they can be found, are

THE MOUNT

Figure 11.2 Map of Crowhurst Park estate on Blackhorse Hill dated 1744.

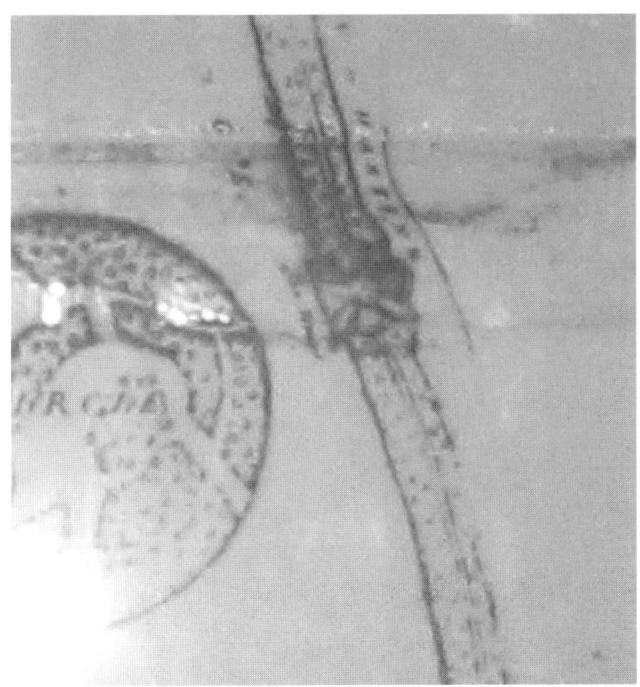

Figure 11.3 Shows enlarged view of 'The Mount' by the Hastings road (now A2100). Appendix 8 discusses its significance. *(Credit Colin Simmons)*

important evidence for the archaeologists to examine. *The Carmen*, in beautiful lines written of the Battle of Hastings, recalls the dramatic aftermath of the battle and the gruesome task of burying the dead:

> After the glorious light of the sun began to shine and cleanse the world of brooding darkness, the duke surveyed the field, and taking up the bodies of his fallen, he buried them in the bosom of the earth.

The unequal treatment implied here: taking up the bodies of his fallen, may not have been to dishonour the English dead, but more a question of practicality. The battle lasted some nine hours of great brutality and inevitably resulted in a large death toll; how many is impossible to know given there are no reliable figures for those taking part on each side in the first place. Anyway, at least we should expect there to be Norman burials, at or near, the battlefield and determination of this location should finally determine the battlefield site.

Next we look at the possible relevance of The Mount[8] to the battlefield site, and whether it might contain burials.

Chapter 12

Burials

Although the place of King Harold's interment has no bearing on the subject of this book – the location of the battle – it is something that has puzzled historians for centuries and the subject merits inclusion here.

The Carmen's account of Harold's burial merits attention because it was written shortly after the event and although his accounts cannot always be relied upon, on this occasion there is no reason not to:

> Harold's dismembered body he [William] gathered together, and wrapped what he had gathered in fine purple linen, and returning to his camp by the sea [the Port of Hastings] he bore it with him, that he might carry out the customary funeral rites.

A Viking style of funeral[1] – perhaps.

The Carmen tells that William had earlier rejected a request from Harold's grieving mother to purchase the body and instead 'commanded the body to be buried in the earth on the high summit of a cliff' (by the sea presumably).

Some accounts have it that after Harold's death, his body was brought to Waltham Abbey, Essex, for burial near to the High Altar. But intriguingly, in 1954 during repair works in Holy Trinity Church, Bosham, West Sussex, a grave containing the remains of a man without a head, a leg and part of another leg, was found in a stone coffin. The scene in the Bayeux Tapestry showing Harold being struck on the thigh by a mounted knight, and Wace's description of a knight 'striking him on the thick of his thigh down to the bone', is commensurate with the mutilated remains found, although contrary to *The Carmen*'s account saying it was buried on a high cliff.

That Bosham had been the principal home of Harold and he had sailed from that port in 1064 to visit Normandy before his crowning two years later, raises the tantalising possibility that his remains had been moved there for burial after his death at the Battle of Hastings or even moved from Waltham Abbey.

But our main interest here is what became of the dead following the battle, as the burial site might lead us to the battle site.

Wace writes of it:

> They bore the bodies [the Saxons] to their villages, and interred them at churches; and clerks and priests of county were ready, and, at the request of their friends, took the bodies that were found and prepared graves and lay them therein.

This may be so in some instances where homes were nearby, but unlikely in general with the Saxon army having been drawn from across the country – meaning battlefield burials were more likely. *The Carmen* has the Saxon dead at 10,000 just from the 'feint' incident:

> Those who feigned flight wheeled on the pursuers and forced them, held in check, to flee from death. A great part fell there (but part in close order stood fast), for indeed ten thousand suffered destruction in that place.

Perhaps this figure is exaggerated given the propensity of the author to curry favour with the duke by talking up the numbers. Nevertheless, Saxon deaths must have been large. Later in the text, *The Carmen* relates that the Saxon dead were not buried but left on the field:

> The corpses of the English, strewn upon the ground, he left to be devoured by worms and wolves, by birds and dogs.

BURIALS

As we have seen, the Norman dead received battlefield burials (we repeat *The Carmen*):

> After the glorious light of the sun began to shine and cleanse the world of brooding darkness, the duke surveyed the field, and taking up the bodies of his fallen, he buried them in the bosom of the earth.

Although William had inflicted a crushing defeat, the duke, himself weakened, had no idea what other forces he might still have to face and following the chase of the remnants of the Saxon army through Beauport Wood, returned to his stronghold at Hastings where the army remained for a fortnight according to *The Carmen*. Maybe the burials were carried out during this period.

Nick Austin has searched for burial sites in his quest to confirm his theory that the battle was fought at Crowhurst. The videos and ground radar images he produced can be viewed online, but for obvious reasons their location has not been revealed. As far as it is understood, the results have not been examined by experts, and fields nearby have been used to dispose of the cattle culled during foot and mouth outbreaks. These could easily be mistaken for human burials.

Chapter 13

The Battlefield that wasn't

A major obstacle to researching the Battle of Hastings and its whereabouts is the all-pervading presence of the abbey remains at Battle and the adjacent fields where the historic event is claimed to have taken place. To challenge the tradition is seen as heresy and to risk professional suicide.

If the battle was at Blackhorse Hill, we need to reconcile this with the presence of the abbey ruins 2 miles away to the west. English Heritage claims that the armies of King Harold and William the Conqueror clashed at the Battle of Hastings and you can stand on the very site where this decisive struggle was fought and that William the Conqueror founded Battle Abbey on the exact spot where Harold died, as penance for the bloodshed of the Norman Conquest.

The ancient *Chronicle of Battle Abbey* is the provenance of this 'truth':

> William built another monastery near Hastings, dedicated to St. Martin, which was also called Battle, because there the principal church stands on the very spot, where, as they report, Harold was found in the thickest heaps of the slain.

And William of Malmesbury, writing at about the same time, also has the battle at the abbey site. Whether William of Malmesbury was taking his lead from the abbots at Battle Abbey is unknown.

The Battle Abbey estate, purchased for the nation from the Webster family by English Heritage in 1976, has been a major tourist attraction ever since. The Websters had owned it since 1715 having

THE BATTLEFIELD THAT WASN'T

purchased it from the Sixth Viscount Montague. His antecedent, Sir Anthony Browne, the King's Master of Horse, had acquired it by gift from King Henry VIII in 1538 following the Dissolution of the Monasteries.

Battle Abbey was founded as a Benedictine monastery soon after the Battle of Hastings on the urgings of King William's monks, as penance for the bloodshed that fateful day. The abbey church was finished in 1094; the cloisters and outer court and other works followed.

Clearly, Sir William Browne had no respect for the 'historic battle site', even if he was aware of its history: he demolished the abbey church, chapter house and parts of the cloister and reconstructed the complex as the palatial residence visitors see today. All that remains are parts of the abbey foundations and the ruins of the monks' dormitory.

When the abbey complex and its lands became established as the traditional battlefield is unknown, but English Heritage admits visitors to the site promoting it as such, having a marker for the actual spot where King Harold met his end nearly a thousand years ago, with a stone laid into the grass where the abbey altar was supposed to have once stood. A Mr Vidler writing in 1841 (*Gleanings Reflecting Battel and its Abbey*, Longman) discounts this:

> William of Malmesbury says that the assertion of it [the altar stone] being on the spot were [*sic*] Harold was killed is a mere invention of the monks.

The author has been unable, so far, to locate this 'Malmesbury' quote.

Whilst this writer believes the evidence demonstrates the Battle of Hastings actually took place up on the Telham Ridge at Blackhorse Hill, he does not presume to dismiss lightly the traditional battle site at Battle Abbey. Clearly, the site being advanced in this book has to contend with this tradition and here we consider how Battle Abbey, wrongly, came to be the established site.

Readers will, in the end, have to weigh the evidence presented in these pages against the words of the *Chronicle of Battle Abbey*'s establishment of the customary site, but it cannot rest there standing in the way of the consideration of any alternative site, when it is unlikely that King Harold would have ever contemplated defending a weak position such as that offered by the abbey site. It is the claims of the monks in the *Chronicle of Battle Abbey*[1] (written a century after the battle) that William while readying his army on the morning before battle had promised to build an abbey on the Battle Abbey site, that we address here. There is no doubt William did promise an abbey on the battle site, done in the heat of the moment before the battle to boost morale:

The *Chronicle* gives the provenance to William's promise:

> Having arrived at a hill called Hechlande situated in the direction of Hastings, while they were helping one another on with their armour, there was brought forth a coat of mail for the duke to put on, and by accident it was handed to him the wrong side foremost. Those who stood by and saw this cursed it as an unfortunate omen, but the duke's sewer again bade them good cheer, and declared that this was a token of good fortune, ... The duke, perfectly unmoved, put on the mail with a placid countenance, and uttered these memorable words: 'I know, my dearest friends, that if I had any confidence in omens, I ought on no account to go to battle today. ... Wherefore, now, secure of his aid, and in order to strengthen the hand and courage of you, who for my sake are about to engage in in this conflict, I make a Vow, that upon this place of battle I will found a suitable free Monastery.

In this chapter we look at the reliability of the *Chronicle*'s assertion that the site of the battle was where the abbey ultimately came to be built.

How have the two proponents of an alternative battle site dealt with this conundrum? The first, John Grehan,[2] does not have to concern himself with the issue at his Caldbec Hill site because the battle was more mobile in the latter stages after the shield wall perimeter had been broken into than popular understanding makes out. Caldbec Hill, being in such close proximity (half mile distant) to the abbey site, can be considered part of the greater battlefield, and within the vicinity of the traditional battle site.

Nick Austin, the other proponent, justifies his rejection of the *Chronicle of Battle Abbey* account being proof that the abbey site was the site for the Battle of Hastings, on the grounds that the abbey had no documents to prove it and that forgeries had instead been made. He said the abbey was 'in trouble [when taxes were demanded] because they had no document that they could rely on, so they had to insert some information into that document and every time they inserted it they said it's tradition [that their abbey was the site of the battle] that this happened'.[3] This sounds (to this author) a rational reason for rejecting the monks' claim.

Researcher Eleanor Searle published a paper: 'Battle Abbey and Exemptions: The Forged Charters'[4] in which she probed the reliability of the several royal and episcopal charters produced between 1155 and 1215 that formed part of the *Chronicle of Battle Abbey*.

Students and readers interested in Anglo-Norman franchises and church history will want to read the full treatise. But here we must limit ourselves to an outline of the issues that lead to a serious breach between the abbot and monks on the one hand, and the Bishop of Chichester on the other, and how that long-running dispute impacts on the legitimacy of Battle Abbey's claim to being the true site of the Battle of Hastings.

The issue was Battle Abbey's right to exemption from subjection to bishops, in particular the bishops of Chichester (i.e. the monks' claim that William promised: 'I will found a suitable free Monastery'). Although a minor breach in exemptions occurred the year following the abbey's dedication in 1094, peace reigned for the next forty years and the abbey continued to enjoy its exemptions even though the abbey lay within the jurisdiction of Chichester Cathedral. This relaxed situation could continue because, according to the *Chronicle*, abbots cooperated with the bishops of Chichester and presumably, bishops in turn did not insist too forcefully on their rights being upheld, even if they understood them.

However, matters were about to be put to the test when Abbot Walter de Luci (1139–71), refused to continue obeying summons to attend Synod and at the same time Bishop Hilary (1147–69) began demanding rights from the Abbey. As the dispute developed, the abbot failed to offer documentary proof of the exemptions to the bishop because, and this is important for our story, either he did not actually have any or did not want to disclose for unknown reasons, otherwise he would surely have done so.

In November 1154, Hilary excommunicated the abbot after obtaining the Pope's support for his action. But the abbot had influence in high places, for his brother Richard de Luci was justiciar and an important part of the king's administrative machine who was able to persuade Archbishop Theobald to get Bishop Hilary to retract.

Abbot Walter then produced his first document[5] to support his claim, with an exemption clause included[6] ready to present to King Henry II who had just succeeded to the throne following the death of King Stephen on 25 October 1154. What followed was an outburst of stunned disbelief, the king and his advisers suspecting forgery. Searle has extensively studied this document and comes to the same conclusion, showing it to be a forgery on four counts – listed at the end of this chapter.

The dispute was resolved for the time being at a hearing in Colchester in May 1157 in the presence of the king, the archbishop, the chancellor, the justiciar and other interested parties where the offending charter and two other charters were presented (Searle finds another three to be forgeries as well). The king ruled in favour of the abbot and abbey, and Bishop Hilary was forced to renounce all claims.

That was not the end of it though; from 1157 until 1215 another seven charters created by the abbey were examined by Searle and shown to be forgeries, including one claiming exemption from taxes demanded by the exchequer. Searle does not commit specifically to ruling out the abbey being the site of the Battle of Hastings, but what she did conclude was that:

> [S]o much doubt has been cast upon so many of the Battle Abbey charters that none can now be used with confidence as evidence of the acts of Anglo-Norman kings.

Searle, in summarising her paper, believed that William I:

> very probably did forbid any outside interference with the monks who were building the abbey and very probably issued a writ to this effect to his secular ministers. But he did not issue a charter of exemption from episcopal authority, nor did the foundation charter of William II include such exemptions.

The *Chronicle*, with its account of the battle compiled late in the twelfth century, 100 years and more after the battle, and incorporating the forged charters in a clumsy attempt to have what was not granted, recognised, had the incidental effect of creating the oral tradition of Battle Abbey being the battle site – but the systematic fraudulence means no trust can be attached to this tradition.

So having this in mind, let us look again, using a different translation, at how the *Chronicle* accounts for the abbey being sited where it is and try to work out what really happened.

As we have seen from the *Chronicle*'s account, the abbey's founding has its origins during the preparations on the morning of the battle. It is pretty clear that William was behind the founding of the abbey, but did he make this Vow and was it remembered in such detail when the *Chronicle* was compiled 100 years or so later?[7]

The *Chronicle* continues that there was no progress on the abbey as the duke was occupied with 'numerous and weighty affairs', and it was not until 1072 that his work of conquering England was complete. He then departed to Normandy to deal with pressing matters, leaving his half-brother, Bishop Odo, to run the kingdom. William, we are told, then put the work in the hands of the monk, William Faber, following constant reminders from him, and told him to bring over four brethren from his abbey in Marmoutier.

But things soon go awry when the monks from Marmoutier declare the battle site unsuitable for an abbey and instead commence work at a 'place lower down on the western side of the hill', building some 'little dwellings'.[8] But William was having none of this, so we are told in the *Chronicle*. In spite of protestations that the site he wanted was 'upon a hill with a parched soil, dry, and destitute of water', he demanded that the abbey be built on the site of the battle anyway – meaning upon a hill with parched soil, dry, and destitute of water and of course higher up (from where they were building) on the eastern side of the hill (really a ridge).

The *Chronicle* continues: 'Thus at length the foundations were laid'. But 'the building work went on but slowly' on account of building fraud and importantly, we are told, the king never visited the construction and died without ever doing so.

It is not surprising that William never visited the abbey works, and it helps to show why this was by looking at his travel and occupations in his twenty-one years following the Battle of Hastings:[9]

1066–1072	subjugated the rest of England and built castles to reinforce his rule.
1076	to Normandy for several years on the Breton Campaign.
1080	in Normandy until peace with the Bretons was patched up.
1081–1087	in Normandy but with frequent visits to England.

THE BATTLEFIELD THAT WASN'T

1081–1082   in England and Normandy for two years – on Welsh campaigns, meeting with his half-brother, Bishop Odo, on the Isle of Wight and removing him to prison in Normandy for misrule of England during his absence.

1083   in Normandy after death of his wife, Matilda, and at the siege of St Sussane.

1083–1084   in England raising taxes and carrying out 'scorched earth' in the east against expected Danish attack.

1085–1086   in England for the 'great survey' and compilation of the *Domesday Book* with his active involvement.

1087   to Normandy for the final time, dying following a horseriding accident while fighting in a border dispute in the Vexin and interred in Normandy.

The abbey was only consecrated in 1094, seven years after his death. Considering the active life William lead, continuously countering rebellion, defending lands against neighbouring encroachment and extending his domain, is it any wonder that William never got to review progress on the abbey?

So what Happened?

Unless some ancient account turns up in an archive, it is unlikely we shall ever know the full story of how the abbey came to be built at the site where its remains now lie. But considering the glaring unsuitability of the Battle Abbey site as a defensive position for a weakened and depleted army that had just dashed from a brutal and bloody battle at Stamford Bridge yet were able to hold out all day against massed cavalry, could the abbey really be at the site of the battle?

There was little progress, if any, building the abbey until late in William's reign; have we a king with little interest in a memorial abbey or the time to busy himself with it, or was the idea, just like much of the *Chronicle*, a fabrication? The monks, we see, were also not especially concerned with their abbey being built on the battlefield, and may actually not have wanted it there for obvious reasons. What they needed was offered by the lower site where the town of Battle now stands, a site not lacking water and not so barren, as at Blackhorse Hill, so they could cultivate crops, construct fish ponds and raise animals. Mr Vidler, again, in *Gleanings Reflecting Battel and its Abbey* on the subject of the abbey's siting seems to agree:

> The monks seem to have been more anxious about their own comfort and convenience than they were to fulfil the intentions of their sovereign and benefactor. They coveted valleys where the soil was richer, and water more plentiful, than on the spot where the victory was gained.

Vidler does not say here where the battle was fought, but clearly he did not believe it was where the abbey ruins lay. The *Chronicle* was constructed for ulterior motives and cannot be relied upon to inform us about the battle's location.

In trying to gauge what happened, we should be conscious that the monks who built the abbey were an earlier generation to those responsible for the *Chronicle* (and its forgeries). They were carefully crafting a story for their own ends, although the story, no doubt, had elements of truth to it.

It is reasonable then to suppose that the monks called over from Marmoutier when the site for the abbey was being prepared, had had no role and little interest in the battle that occurred several years before and simply built the abbey where it best suited them. At that time, the Church was all-powerful and the king would probably defer to the monks' wishes, if he got involved at all. The Church was virtually untouchable,[10] and it, having the backing of the Pope and knowing William would need the Church for the salvation of his soul for all the blood spilt, left them to it.

Finally, some readers may also wonder whether English Heritage scrutinised Eleanor Searle's analysis of the *Chronicle of Battle Abbey*, presented above in outline, before purchasing the abbey and complex for the nation, or whether they were unaware of her work that had been published some eight years before the purchase.

Searle's Four Counts of Charter Forgery

1. William I. Ref: BM.[11] Harleian 83 A12

This charter was presented to Henry II in 1155, the year following his accession, for confirmation. Searle states it was most likely forged soon after the death of Stephen.

Indications of forgery:

- The writing is not contemporary with William I, it being mid-twelfth century.
- The method of sealing is not contemporary with William I. The foot of the charter is folded and the seal tag threaded through the resulting double thickness; a method not seen before 1120.
- Although the document had been sealed, the seal itself is now missing, so the authenticity of the seal cannot be checked.
- The list of witnesses is impossible; William Fitz Osbern had died by 1071.

2. William II. Ref: BM. Egerton Charter 22II

This charter was claimed as a foundation charter by the monks of Battle Abbey, but its writing was mid-twelfth century. Furthermore, the Latin *ego* followed directly with *nobis* cannot be from the eleventh century – it was an error common to the mid-twelfth century when the document was first presented.

3. Henry I

The original charter is lost and the analysis has been carried out on a copy. Searle states:

> It cannot be accepted as genuine in the form it was shown to Henry II; none of the addressees and witness, bishop Seffrid of Chichester ... know anything of the exemption[12] confirmed by the king [William I].

4. William I. BM. Add. Charter 70980

The writing is mid-twelfth century and marked by exaggerated ascenders[13] in the top line. The document is sealed with a known forged seal of William I[14] that was made available to several monasteries as well as Battle Abbey monastery.

These four forged charters were the totality of those brought before Henry between 1155 and 1157 claiming exemption for Battle Abbey on the grounds they were foundation charters.

There were other forgeries made by Battle Abbey after 1157, which are not detailed here. However, Searle provides detail of a further four made between 1157 and 1174, plus three from 1200–1215.

APPENDICES

Appendix 1

The Sedlescombe Hoard

One August day in 1876, a man digging a drain in a field in the village of Sedlescombe, East Sussex, unearthed a small, much-corroded, broken iron pot containing old silver pennies in the remains of a leather bag, all of King Edward the Confessor, whose long reign came to an end on 5 January 1066.

An article in the *Numismatic Chronicle* in 1878 describes the hoard as pint-sized and of four different sorts. The *Chronicle* continued, 'There were none of the early types of this king's pennies in the hoard', meaning they were all minted either just before, or not long before, the Battle of Hastings. The hoard has not been kept together[1] and an R. Dolley, in a feature for the British Numismatic Society publication in the 1960s reported having seen thirty-two coins from the collection and attests: 'This great treasure,[2] almost certainly part of the bullion reserve of the Hastings mint at the time of the Norman invasion, was widely dispersed.' Dolley relates that the coins were of pristine brightness and it was clear that before concealment many of the coins had changed hands no more than once or twice.

What is of significance about this find for us is that the old Roman road to East Sussex, a branch of the road to Dover (Watling Street) at Rochester, passed through the village of Sedlescombe as Kent Street. King Harold's army, as we have seen earlier, would have taken it in the dash from Stamford Bridge to London to confront Duke William of Normandy. Sedlescombe is just 3 miles north of the battle site on the spur from Telham Ridge at Blackhorse Hill. The manor of Sedlescombe, according to Mark Anthony Lower's[3] *History of Sussex*, published in 1876, 'passed from Earl Godwin to his son Harold [later King Harold II], and after the Conquest it was held of the Earl of Eu [Walter Fitz Lambert]'; Harold having holdings in Sussex and knowing the area would have been in a good position to choose the best base there.

Although the Saxon army did not have such formidable formations as the Normans, its commanders were well versed in tactics and strategy and knew how to use the weapons they had – after all, they had had to deal with Viking invasions over the two previous centuries. They knew not to throw themselves into battle without careful planning. They knew to form up well before meeting the enemy, and like William, would have established a base camp to do this. Late arrivals from the battle at Stamford Bridge and reinforcements arriving from across the country could be briefed, perhaps given arms and directed to the front from this base. It would, no doubt, have been established well before the battle, even at the time the Saxon army was forced to march north to deal with the Norwegian army. Weapons, food and water could have been held there and conveyed to the front as the battle raged on – this was no 'off-the-cuff' arrangement. This would explain why the king had left 'an entrance on each of three sides'.[4]

If this base camp was at Sedlescombe, and there was no other settlement better suited for the needs, then it is easy to understand how a pot of money came to be buried there. Medieval armies were made up from levies and needed paying; ready cash was always carried to purchase everything else that was required. No doubt there were other stashes and some could still remain to be found. Although King Harold had probably hoped to win the battle, he would have made contingency arrangements for a defeat; that is probably how a pot of money came to be hidden at Sedlescombe.

Beyond this being an interesting adjunct to our search for the battle site, it is in line with the general shape of the story and the contention that the Saxon army approached it down the old Roman road and came nowhere near to the traditional site at Battle Abbey.

Figure App 1.1 Two Edward the Confessor coins from the hoard found at Sedlescombe.

Appendix 2

Comparison of Battlefields – Traditional with Blackhorse Hill

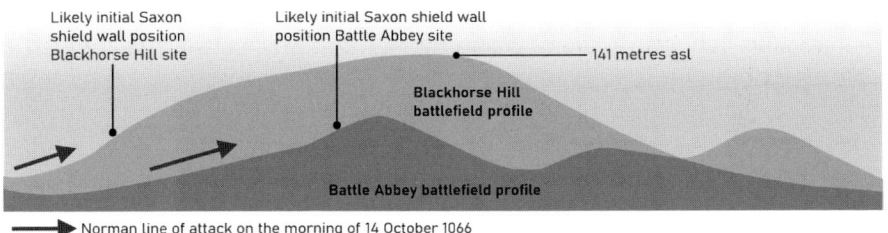

Figure App 2.1 Profile overlay of battlefields at the traditional (Battle Abbey) site and Blackhorse Hill.

This profile overlay Figure App 2.1, above for Battle Abbey and the Blackhorse Hill battlefield sites[1] shows the relative advantages and disadvantages presented by each. If King Harold and his lieutenants had selected Blackhorse Hill in a conscious decision in preference to the Battle Abbey site, then they chose well. In fact, there is no better site within reasonable striking distance of the Norman encampment at Hastings port. It could not have been a decision made on the spur of the moment as the main Saxon army was arriving over the night of 13/14 October, just before and even after the battle had started – the site must have been pre-selected. The Blackhorse Hill site is militarily superior for the Saxons in that:

- Firstly, the attackers had to contend with a much steeper slope pushing back against the shield wall – typically 24 per cent (excepting at the east side of the defensive perimeter) against typically 7 per cent at the Battle Abbey site. Furthermore, the height to be climbed by the Norman army was almost twice that at the Battle Abbey site. So long as the defenders could prevent outflanking manoeuvres, then the Normans below would be struggling against gravity as well as the enemy. The Normans faced exhaustion and defeat.

- Secondly, flanking movements against the Saxon shield wall, lying along the contour and looping northward on each side and probably extending into the woods from which they had occupied the heights, would have been virtually impossible to execute. On the other hand, the Battle Abbey site lies along a ridge where the terrain does not provide a natural barrier against outflanking. The mobile Norman cavalry units would have easily circumvented the Saxon line, attacked the rear and rolled up the Saxons in short order. The battle could not have lasted until dusk.
- Finally, at Blackhorse Hill, the extent of rising ground beyond the shield wall defences before falling off northwards is approximately seven times greater, at 546 yards, than at Battle Abbey, at just 70 yards – meaning the defenders can count on more time, if being pushed back. This would have increased the chance of staying in the field until nightfall when Duke William, faced with more Saxon troops arriving, would have essentially ended his opportunity of conquering England and becoming king. But, of course, the disintegration of the Saxon army before dusk meant this advantage did not present itself and instead the Saxon army's battle ended in rout.

That the Saxon army failed in the end has been much written about; that King Harold had little or no cavalry should not have mattered at the highly defendable Blackhorse Hill site. But it was the tactics of the Norman commanders that won out in the end. Having failed to make serious inroads into the shield wall for most of the day, the invading army after two or three feints, together with the pressure from Norman arms, caused the Saxon line to collapse following their ill-advised pursuit of what they thought was a defeated Norman army.

That the fight endured unusually long for a medieval battle, taking up nine hours of the day, from 9 a.m. till dusk before the Saxon army

COMPARISON OF BATTLEFIELDS

was beaten, is testimony, not only to the resilience and bravery of the Saxons, but to the skilful selection of the Blackhorse Hill site.

The traditional site at Battle Abbey fails in so many respects. The cavalry advantage held by the Normans would not have been impeded on the short gentle slopes up to the shield wall. And the weak flank defences would also have contributed to defeat and the battle would have been over early.

Finally, all armies (especially its cavalry section) require large quantities of water to stave off dehydration and loss of endurance. The OS map of Blackhorse Hill shows several ponds, relics it is understood, from medieval iron workings. Whether there were ponds at the time of the battle is unknown, but as we have seen, the monks, looking for a site for an abbey, said the soil was parched, dry and destitute of water, so they would have had to transport water to the site – the Normans, we know, brought a baggage train to the battle and presumably so did the Saxons.

Appendix 3

Consideration of the Traditional Battle Abbey Battlefield, the Norman Route and March Time from Wilting Camp

This 'what if' examination looks at what the Norman army would have faced had they had to march to the battlefield at the Battle Abbey location. The only feasible route to the battlefield is shown as a red line in Figure App 3.3. The route height profile, Figure App 3.1, follows the 25m contour avoiding the undulating ground of a direct route, shown in height profile (Figure App 3.2. below) or the boggy ground following the banks of Combe Haven.

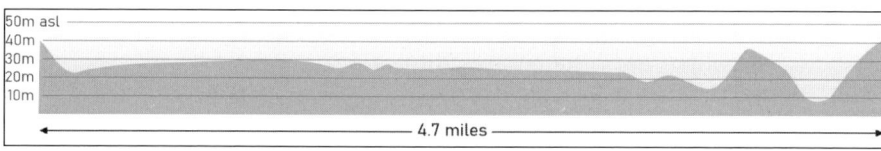

Figure App 3.1 The only practical route for the Norman army to the traditional battlefield.

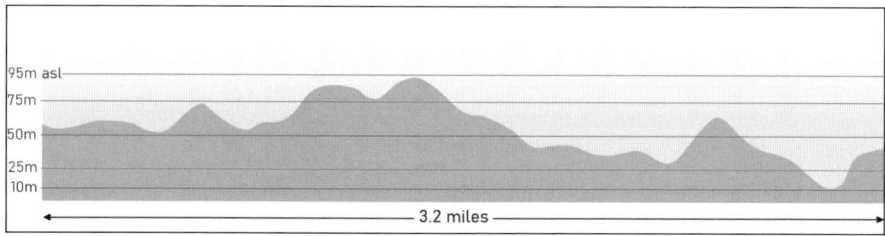

Figure App 3.2 Wilting Farm to the Battle Abbey traditional battlefield terrain profile direct, 'as the crow flies'.

CONSIDERATION OF THE TRADITIONAL BATTLE

This detour would have been at a cost, a longer march of 4.7 miles. At the best speed of travel of 2mph determined in Chapter 8, and allowing a factor for 'wander', bunching and forming up, it would have taken over three hours to arrive at the traditional battlefield at the Battle Abbey site ready at the start line, militating against the traditional site.

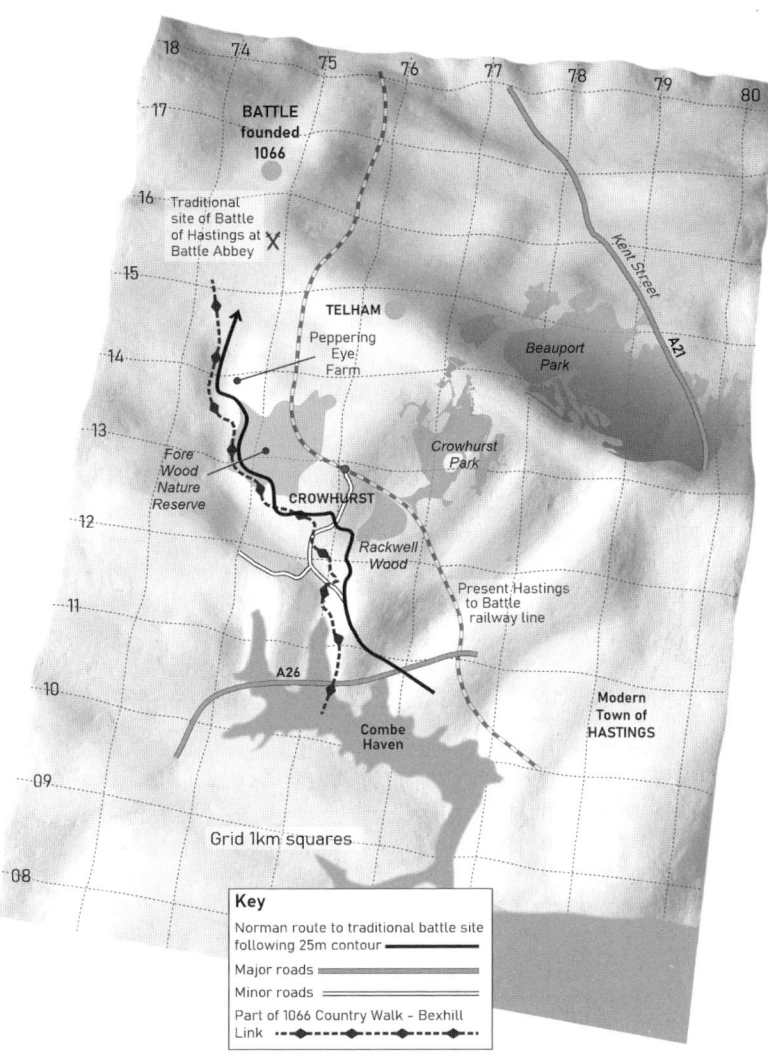

Figure App 3.3 Wilting Farm to the Battle Abbey traditional site terrain profile following the 25m contour for most of the distance (on the same scale as Figure App 3.2, opposite). See colour plate section.

Appendix 4

The Wastings

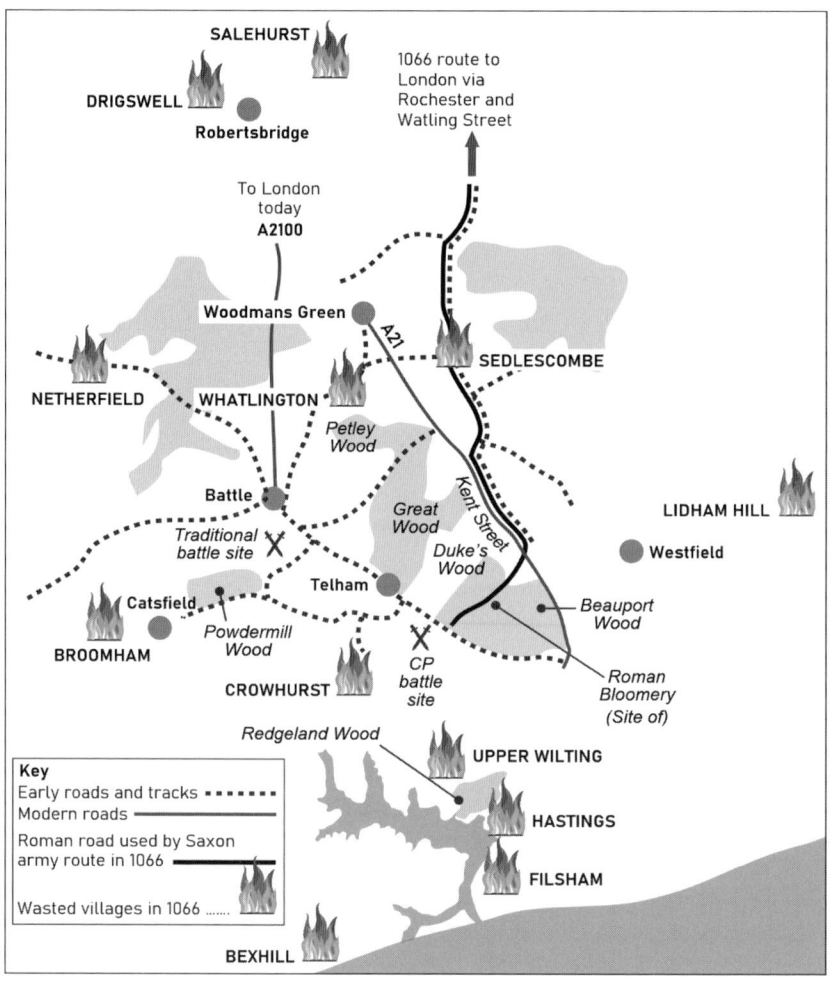

Figure App 4.1 Map of East Sussex showing the area wasted by the Norman army before and after the Battle of Hastings. See colour plate section.

THE WASTINGS

Nick Austin has used the 1086 Domesday survey for East Sussex to highlight where the Norman army ravaged the countryside. The map of East Sussex shows the towns and villages that are listed on the survey as 'wasted' (meaning, essentially, destroyed, as the value at the time of the survey was zero) by the Norman army before and after the Battle of Hastings – note the area around the Norman encampment on the banks of Combe Haven was particularly affected.

The point Austin was making was that the Normans before the battle were mostly marauding (townships wasted indicated on the map by the 'flame' symbols) or occupying strong points around and just to the north of the port of Hastings. The wasted towns much further north, including Hazelhurst (now a 'drowned' settlement), Drigswell and others following the old Roman road route to London, may have been ravaged some time after the battle, because the Norman army moved east from its encampment at Hastings after resting, to take the Saxon fortress at Dover and from there travelled west to circumvent London before taking it. It is important to realise that Pevensey and the area to the west of Combe Haven are free from wasting; according to the Domesday survey – all the activity, agreeing with other parts of this book – was to the east of Combe Haven and Hastings.

Appendix 5

Memorials

Intriguingly, although there have been no authenticated archaeological finds proving a battle took place between Norman and Saxon armies in the greater Hastings area,[1] Ordnance Survey map features bear names related to the battle. Besides The Mount, already discussed in Chapter 12, there are woods in Beauport Park named after Duke William (Duke's Wood) and Bishop Odo (Bishop's Wood), leaders of the Norman army and two hills in the vicinity named Blackhorse Hill. One of these lies between Duke's Wood and the present Battle road,[2] A2100, and the other at the highest point of the Telham escarpment 150m from The Mount.

When these features came to acquire their names remains a mystery. They certainly appear on OS maps of the mid-nineteenth century, so would have been in common usage at that time. This raises the question: why these names commemorating the great battle are at or by the battlefield, and not at the traditional site by Battle Abbey 2 miles to the west?

What is the significance of the name 'Blackhorse Hill'? Horses, as would be expected, feature repeatedly in the Bayeux Tapestry. In fact, there are 135 embroidered on it. Of these 135, thirty-seven are black, and of these, fifteen are seen to be ridden by Duke William and five by Bishop Odo in the battle. This can be determined by the marking of the horses ridden by the duke and his half-brother, Bishop Odo. There are changes in the markings of the horse William rides during the battle, indicating change of mount and agreeing with contemporary accounts telling us he was dismounted twice.

MEMORIALS

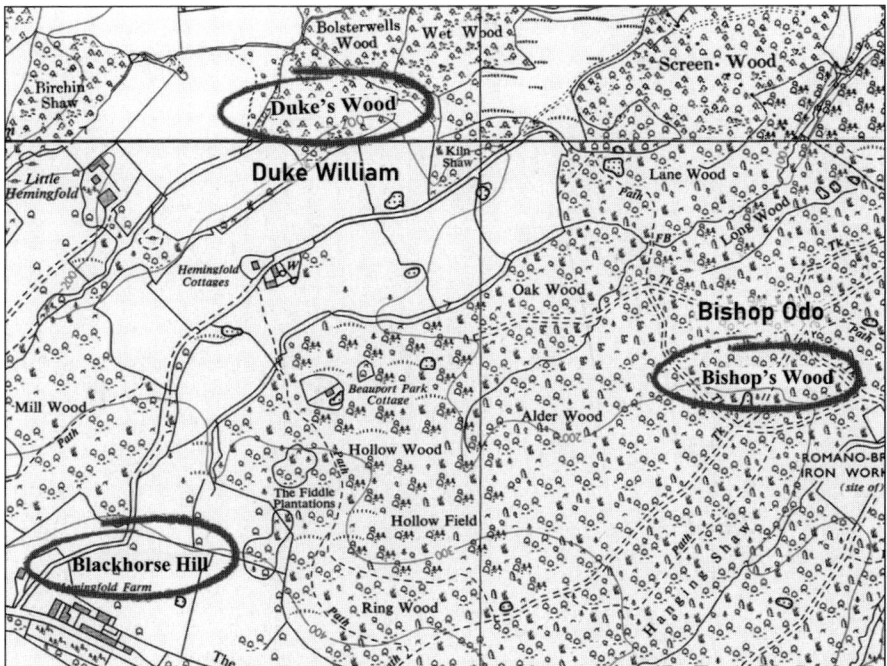

Figure App 5.1 OS 6 miles to the inch 1949–1969 showing geographical features that could be named after Duke William and Bishop Odo.

It is noteworthy that in all twenty scenes where William and Odo are depicted battling on their war horses, the horse is always black. Apart from a couple of scenes where it is difficult to determine who the rider of the black horses is, it seems that only the two brothers are permitted to ride a black horse. The significance of this is unknown: was it just a ruling for the Battle of Hastings, or does it have some meaning in historical terms?

The fact seems to be reflected in the memorials left to the battle seen in the marked-up maps: Figures App 5.1 and 5.2. It is of course unlikely we shall ever learn when these features received their names; whether it was at the time of the battle and formally announced, or whether the names were adopted in later years or even centuries later. But here it is proposed that the location of these related names is evidence that the battle took place in the vicinity of those features, i.e. Blackhorse Hill.

1066: THE LOST HASTINGS BATTLEFIELD

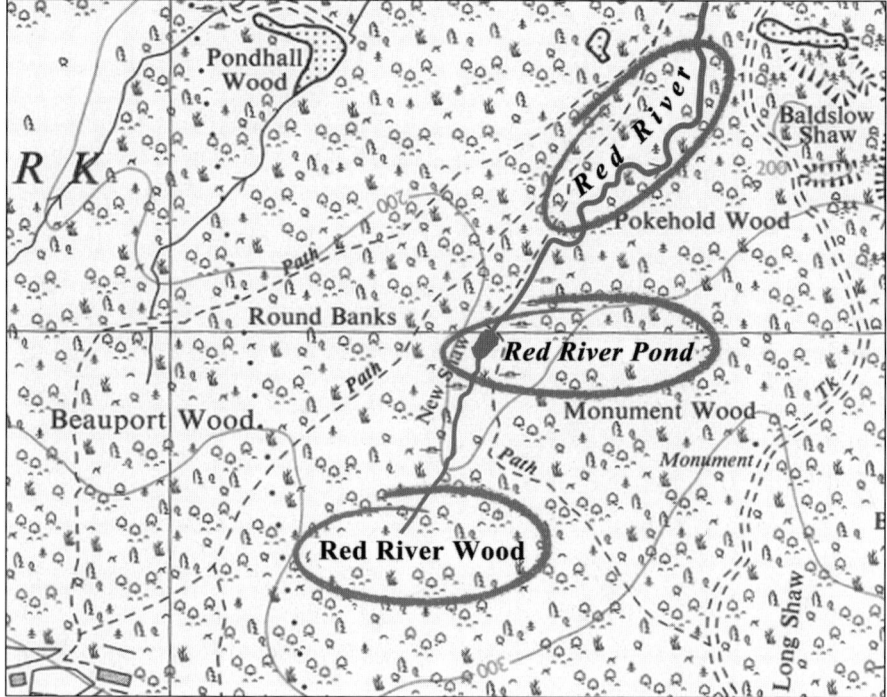

Figure App 5.2. OS 6 miles to the inch 1949–1969 showing Red River, Red River Wood and Red River Pond.

There is one further geographical feature, named on the map above, Figure App 5.2, that is worth addressing: a river, more a stream, called Red River at the eastern end of Beauport Wood. On this map there is also a Red River Wood, the wood from which the stream emanates and lower down the slope there is a Red River Pond. In Chapter 10, the *Chronicle of Battle Abbey* describes the bitter fight between pursuing Normans and fleeing Saxons at a 'dreadful precipice'. It would be tempting to believe that the dreadful precipice was the ravine through which the Red River flows and that it gets its name from the blood spilt as the defeated army fought to escape through the woods to Kent Street. But it is also possible that the river is named from the colour of the water which, after rains, sometimes flows reddish – caused by iron deposits, which proliferate through the area, leaching out. It will probably be impossible to ever know the provenance.

Appendix 6

Archaeology

English Heritage[1] operates Battle Abbey and the battlefield complex in East Sussex. It is an important attraction with over 100,000 visitors annually, but remarkably, no archaeological evidence consistent with a battle in 1066 has ever been found.

The Abbey Museum in the gatehouse exhibits a collection of medieval finds from the vicinity but there is nothing contemporary from the battle. This lack of remains is usually put down to the battlefield having been scoured by victorious soldiers and local scavengers searching for anything of worth – metalwork from broken armour, weapons or bits of weapons, personal items and clothing, anything that could be sold or repaired and reused.

Additionally, they say, anything that was not recovered will have deteriorated beyond recognition over the millennium since the battle and anything that might be datable will now be below the surface covered with alluvial deposits.

In 2013, English Heritage, wishing to strengthen the case for the abbey site brought in Channel 4[2] *Time Team* archaeologists to investigate the site and examine rival claims for the battlefield location. They soon encountered difficulties with items lost by people and horses after modern-day battle re-enactments staged over the years. They brought in diggers to overcome the problem by scraping off a layer of topsoil to eliminate recent debris confusing ground radar so they could be fairly certain that anything then excavated was not modern.

Veteran presenter Sir Tony Robinson fronted the investigation for *Time Team*'s three-day dig. Cutting-edge technology, including high-powered metal detectors were employed in the search of the supposed site, but nothing contemporary with the battle was found. However, English Heritage's custodian Roy Porter was not moved, insistent on the site being the right site: 'We have always maintained that the Abbey is built on the site of the battle because sources dating back to the early 12th Century state that.'[3]

Next, *Time Team* moved to check out Caldbec Hill, the first of the two alternative sites for the battle proposed by military historian John Grehan. On Caldbec Hill, part of an east/west ridge half a mile to the north of the Battle Abbey site, *Time Team* ran metal detectors across 30,000 square feet of the site and found nothing. Then, Nick Austin was invited to defend his site at Crowhurst, a site a mile or so south-east of the abbey site. But rather ill-advisedly he brought along a find he had not had professionally authenticated, claiming it might be a piece of a Norman helmet – twenty years of painstaking research on the old Port of Hastings and the Battle of Hastings was dismissed out of hand, the expert rejecting the find as probably a metal hoop from a barrel or bucket.

However, *Time Team*'s efforts at Battle Abbey succeeded spectacularly in protecting the tradition of the site, prevailing over its plausible rival sites – for the time being. In fact, it couldn't be better: although no archaeology consistent with the traditional site was found, rival claims at the Caldbec Hill and Crowhurst battlefield sites were dealt a virtual death blow by the team.

Time Team Battle employed lidar aerial imaging technology, revealing that 'Harold must have chosen Battle [of course it received its name after the battle] to stop William escaping the Hastings peninsula'.[4] Better still, the battlefield, centred on a mini-roundabout in the centre of the town of Battle, cannot now contradict the story because the 'battlefield' is built over, precluding serious excavational work happening there in the future, although there is always the hope something might turn up in somebody's back garden.

English Heritage was delighted by the lidar scan, with its spectacular colour display of the town of Battle, claiming it confirmed the strategic value of the ridge dominated by the abbey.

ARCHAEOLOGY

Of course, our site, 2 miles away on Blackhorse Hill, has never received the attention of archaeology as far as this writer is aware, but he looks forward to the time when this might change. However, the chances of finding battlefield relics are usually remote because medieval battle sites are usually picked clean by locals after the battle and objects made of iron corrode to iron oxide and leach away into the ground. It is possible that remains lie deep down in the boggy terrain at the Malfosse in the valley below the shield wall site where many men of both sides met their end and it would have been impossible for scavengers to approach safely. The ravines in Beauport Wood where many Norman riders, along with their fleeing foe, fell and were slaughtered, could be the source of archaeological remains – non-ferrous artefacts like buckles and harness pieces.

We have already stated that we do not know if The Mount on Telham Ridge has received an archaeological examination, but if not then the findings in this book should lead to one. However, since the mound was used as a signal beacon, any remains may now be deep down since it is possible the height was raised in later centuries to increase its effectiveness. This possibility should be taken into account should an investigation be carried out.

Finally, a point of possible interest is the recent discovery of corroded weapons near to Stamford Bridge in the East Riding of Yorkshire (see picture to the right) by two metal detectorists. It is probable these finds are from the battle of Stamford Bridge in 1066. Battlefield finds from this period are extremely rare, but it does show that Saxon and Viking weapons used at this time can be preserved in the ground and there ought to have been weapons found at the Battle Abbey battle site. It also means there is all to play for at our Blackhorse Hill battle site.

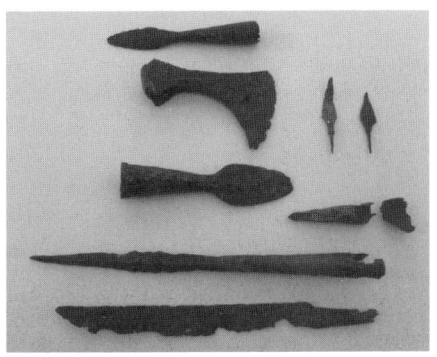

(Picture courtesy Brian Birkett of Stamford Bridge Heritage Society)

Appendix 7

Senlac

Historians, besides attributing the site of the Battle of Hastings to the monks of Battle Abbey having said so, believe that Senlac[1] derives from the French '*sang*', meaning blood or gore and is additional proof that the battle took place at the traditional site by the present town of Battle.

But Orderic Vitalis in his account says: 'the English troops, assembled from all parts of the neighbourhood took post at a place which was anciently called Senlac.' Orderic was born in 1075 in Shrewsbury, and his account was thought to have been written in the first decade of the twelfth century and therefore Senlac being 'ancient', its name pre-dated the Battle of Hastings. It is possible that the name derives from some bloody incident, but not from the blood spilt in 1066.

And again, the name may have come about, as we have seen with 'Red River' in Appendix 5, from the stream at the traditional site turning red from the iron in the soil washed out after rain.

Appendix 8

The Mount Revisited

Figures App 8.1 and 8.2 immediately below, show enlarged images of the Croix pattée – the Christian Cross on the Conqueror's coin. Does the similarity of style between the cross on the king's coin and the cross-shaped mound at The Mount suggest it was a battlefield burial site? Only archaeology could tell, but for the moment the coincidence is stunning.

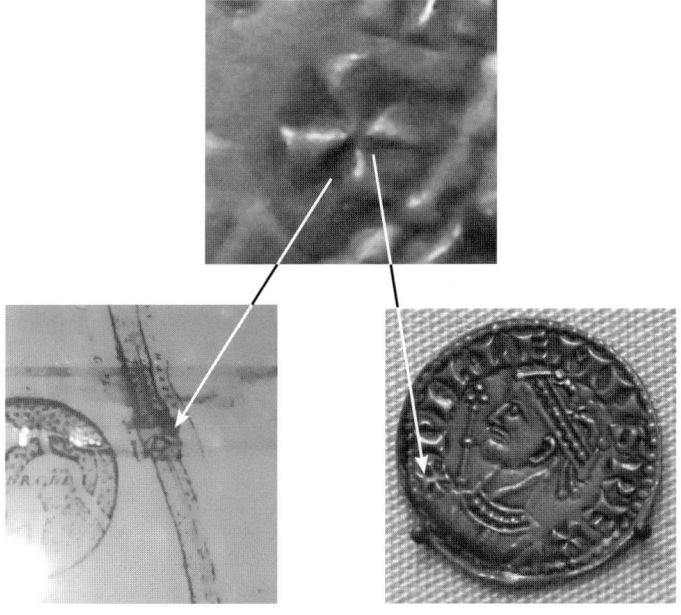

Figure App 8.1 Croix shaped 'Mount' highlighted – refer to the map in Chapter 11 for unretouched image of the Cross.

Figure App 8.2 Coin of William I reign.

Summary of the Evidence for the Battle Site

Chapter 1 page 24, is a review of the features that make for a good medieval defensive battle site. The site at Blackhorse Hill we believe, meets these requirements, making the site itself part of the evidence of the battle having been fought there in 1066.

Norman Fleet Arrives at a Safe Landing Place

The Carmen informs us that the fleet arrived 'at safe landing places', the operative word being 'safe' (Chapter 4, page 58), this rules out a landing on the beaches along the coast. Combe Haven is a safe landing place. *The Carmen* continues after the fleet reached safe landing places: '[the fleet] leaving the sea astern'. This could mean of course that the sea was astern of their beached longboats, but combining this information with 'safe landing places' we have concluded that they were in an 'inland sea' such as Combe Haven.

Later *The Carmen* (Chapter 4, page 58) describes the passage of a comet (also portrayed in the Bayeux tapestries) interpreting it as an omen in favour of Duke William and that the 'land [England] [is] destined for you [the duke] joyfully received you in a calm bay'. What better place than Combe Haven for a calm bay?

Wace described what happened next (Chapter 4, page 59): the 'army passed into the plain with their lances raised'. Whatever one takes the word 'plain' to mean, it clearly eliminates a landing on the beaches

Freepost Plus RTKE-RGRJ-KTTX
Pen & Sword Books Ltd
47 Church Street
BARNSLEY
S70 2AS

DISCOVER MORE ABOUT PEN & SWORD BOOKS

Pen & Sword Books have over 4000 books currently available, our imprints include; Aviation, Naval, Military, Archaeology, Transport, Frontline, Seaforth and the Battleground series, and we cover all periods of history on land, sea and air.

Can we stay in touch? From time to time we'd like to send you our latest catalogues, promotions and special offers by post. If you would prefer not to receive these, please tick this box. ❏

We also think you'd enjoy some of the latest products and offers by post from our trusted partners: companies operating in the clothing, collectables, food & wine, gardening, gadgets & entertainment, health & beauty, household goods, and home interiors categories. If you would like to receive these by post, please tick this box. ❏

We respect your privacy. We use personal information you provide us with to send you information about our products, maintain records and for marketing purposes. For more information explaining how we use your information please see our privacy policy at www.pen-and-sword.co.uk/privacy. You can opt out of our mailing list at any time via our website or by calling 01226 734222.

Mr/Mrs/Ms ....

Address..

Postcode........................... Email address...

Website: www.pen-and-sword.co.uk Email: enquiries@pen-and-sword.co.uk
Telephone: 01226 734555   Fax: 01226 734438
Stay in touch: facebook.com/penandswordbooks or follow us on Twitter @penswordbooks

SUMMARY OF THE EVIDENCE FOR THE BATTLE SITE

under the cliffs to the east of Combe Haven. On the other hand, the land adjacent to Combe Haven, though not exactly a plain in today's understanding of the word, could well be taken to mean the hinterland around the haven.

Duke William's Pre-Battle Base Defensive Location at the Old Port of Hastings

The location of the Norman army's camp before the battle, where they would have trained and waited for the arrival of King Harold and his army, is important for our case. It is important because of the camp's close proximity to the battle site. In Chapter 2, pages 34 to 35, etymological analysis; the remains of earthworks at Upper Wilting Farm; and satellite imaging evidence indicates the location of the Norman defences, constructed following the crossing of the Channel, at the old port of Hastings.

The *Chronicle of Battle Abbey* account has Hastings (meaning the old port of Hastings) by a feature called Hechland (page 34). Using etymological reasoning, we conclude that Hechland and Redgeland, as in Redgeland Wood are the same place. The latter is identifiable on the modern OS map, providing the first clue to the Norman fleet's landing place. This, together with archaeological remains (earthworks) matching the historical record of the Saxon burh at Hastings, has, together with satellite imagery, provided the location of the old port of Hastings.

This is a major stepping stone in our quest to find the 1066 battlefield.

The Roman roads of the area, in use at least until the early nineteenth century, between Combe Haven (the old Saxon port) and the bloomery (iron workings in Beauport Wood) would have benefited the Norman army in its marauding and march to battle on 14 October. This would have been a good reason for Duke William to choose Combe Haven for his forts.

Not Pevensey?

Wace, Chapter 5, page 63 describes a Saxon knight (one no doubt left behind when King Harold marched his army north to oppose the Norwegian invasion, to observe and report on signs of the expected Norman fleet) 'posting himself behind a hill, so that they [the Normans] should not see him watching the arrival of a great fleet'. This makes Pevensey an unlikely landing place since at Pevensey the land around is flat.

Other contemporary accounts in Chapter 4 confirm Hastings as the point of landing.

William Restores the Dismantled Forts (Chapter 6)

The Carmen tells us that William 'restored the dismantled forts which had stood there formerly and set custodians to hold them'.

So there was more than one fort, actually two, an upper fort and a lower fort. Wace tells us that 'before evening had set in, they had finished a fort'. This was the prefabricated fort brought over from France. We have argued that this was the lower fort erected on the banks of Combe Haven on the ruins of the old port of Hastings – they would not have wanted to carry the parts away from the landing area unnecessarily. And Wace tells us the materials were 'cast out of the ships'. He does not mention the materials being carried anywhere else.

The army was at its most vulnerable to attack after landing, hence the reason for the prefabricated 'castle' as the *Anglo-Saxon Chronicle* calls it, for rapid assembly. It had to be built the day of arrival which makes it unlikely they would have had time to carry it elsewhere anyway. We can imagine that the operation had been well rehearsed before departure and everyone would have known their part.

The evidence for the upper fort is a bit more tenuous. We concluded in Chapter 6 that the defensive earthworks at Wilting Farm were the remains of the old Saxon defensive burh at Hastings (perhaps with

SUMMARY OF THE EVIDENCE FOR THE BATTLE SITE

Roman roots – Roman pottery has been found there) and *The Carmen* implies that at the time of the Conquest it was in a suitable state for restoration. The Bayeux Tapestry panel (Figure 6.3) shows tower walls and a sturdy-looking door. This seems as though it could be at the site of the restored Saxon walled burh at Wilting Farm. The chain-mailed soldier departing through the open door is closer to the battlefield than the prefabricated fort lower down the slope. It makes sense, since you would expect the army to marshal as close to the battlefield as possible; the upper fort, rather than at the lower fort.

King Harold Selects his Battlefield – The Highest Hill (Chapter 7)

It is significant that *The Carmen* has King Harold plant his banner 'on the highest point of the summit'. This can be no other location, in the vicinity of Hastings, than Blackhorse Hill (our battlefield). The Mount lies at the highest point.

Later in Chapter 7 we give *The Carmen*'s account of the Saxon army taking possession of the battlefield: 'There was a hill, near the forest and a neighbouring valley and the ground was untilled because of its roughness.' What can be deduced from this is that the battlefield was unforested in 1066 (the ground being untilled), if it wasn't it would have been ruled out as a battlefield. However, there was and still is a forest, a large forest (Beauport Park) near the hill. And, importantly, Blackhorse Hill battlefield has a deep neighbouring valley directly to the west – the topography of the battlefield matching the historical account.

The Normans March to Battle

Wace recounts: the Saxons saw the Norman army approach (viewed from the battlefield or from ground Saxon scouts were occupying) and the Normans 'appeared, advancing over the ridge of rising ground; and the first division of their troops moved along a hill and across a valley'. Wace's description of the terrain the Normans crossed matches what they would have traversed as they set out from the upper fort at Hastings to do battle.

The Battle

Wace writes (page 96) of a fosse (ditch) guarding one side of the army. On the ground at Blackhorse Hill there is a hint of a ditch on one side of the battlefield though Wace also says the field was enclosed. Maybe the rest of the 'enclosure' was the wattle fence mentioned by him on page 99: 'They had built a fence … With their shields, and ash and other wood and had well joined and wattled in the whole work', and if so then there would be no contradiction. William of Poitiers confirms the battle was fought on a hill top: 'The immense English army, …. was arrayed on a hill top.'

Wace (page 103) writes of the Norman baggage:

> The youths and common herd of the camp whose business was not to join battle but to look after the harness and stores, moved off to rising ground. The priests and clerks also ascended a hill there to offer up prayers to God, and watch the events of the battel.

We have identified in Figures 9.2, 9.4 and 9.7 the likely spot for the baggage train. Those in the baggage train believed they were safe on the opposite hill to the west of Blackhorse Hill. Wace recounts that during the fosse event, when the west wing of William's army met with a great slaughter, that 'The varlet who were set to guard the harness began to abandon as they saw loss of the Frenchmen, when thrown back on the fosse. … Being greatly alarmed … they began to quit the harness.'

SUMMARY OF THE EVIDENCE FOR THE BATTLE SITE

This disaster (for the Norman army) at the fosse was the high point for the Saxons. This episode is described in phase 4 of the battle and the location is identified as the marshy ground in the deep valley between Blackhorse Hill battlefield and the hill opposite where the baggage train waited. It was a significant event and topographical evidence for our battle site.

Wace describes (page 114) 'The Englsh [sic] fell back on rising ground.' This is compatible with the rising ground of the battlefield sloping upwards and northwards to the present day A2100 road that passes by The Mount. The ascent ends at the highest point on the 'highest hill' where it begins its descent through the dense woods of Beauport Wood – the scene of the rout.

The Rout

Following the battle and Saxon defeat, the survivors, according to Orderic Vitalis in Chapter 10: the Normans

> galloping onward in hot pursuit fell unawares, horses and armour, into an ancient trench, overgrown and concealed by rank grass and horses rolling over each other, were crushed and smothered. ... This accident restored the routed English, for, perceiving the advantage given them by the mouldering rampart and a succession of ditches.

It describes perfectly the terrain in the wooded area now known as Beauport Park. The illustrations in this chapter show the terrain corresponding to that described.

The Mount

The earliest reference to The Mount appears on a map dated 1744. It is known that it was used as a signal beacon at least as early as the Napoleonic Wars and probably earlier at the time of the Spanish Armada. Chapter 12 discusses this feature and although there is no known evidence of burials, it remains a possibility.

The Mount is on the highest point of the highest hill, exactly the spot where King Harold placed his banner following his occupation of the battle site – what better place for Duke William to bury his dead? *The Carmen* tells us the Norman dead were 'buried in the bosom of the earth'. If The Mount was the place of burial, then they would not have had far to bring the bodies as they would have lain all around on Blackhorse Hill. Perhaps the mound was not as high as it was later in Napoleonic times, it being added to, to increase its elevation for better signalling.

Other clues are the shape (in plan) of The Mount on the 1744 painting. It is symbolically Christian and although today that shape is not so distinct, it still bears a passing resemblance to the Croix pattée. This author has plotted elevations across the feature showing this resemblance. Centuries of erosion, along with the cutting of the A2100 and other disturbances around The Mount, have made it more difficult to make out the shape, but at least part of the cross can be delineated. Appendix 8 shows a contemporary William I coin for comparison (with the Croix). Then there is the suggestion made in Chapter 12 that The Mount was also a monument to William the Conqueror's victory.

The Sedlescombe Hoard (Appendix 1)

The Sedlescombe Hoard consisting of Edward the Confessor coins minted contemporary with or just before the Battle of Hastings, are strong circumstantial evidence for our battle site. The evidence is strong because of the location of the hoard and because the time of minting was just before the battle. The likelihood is that the hoard was hidden by the commanders of the Saxon army before the battle. The purpose, we can surmise, was to retain a source of funding to pay

SUMMARY OF THE EVIDENCE FOR THE BATTLE SITE

surviving troops (and perhaps their widows), and other expenses – they would not have risked taking the money those extra few miles to the battlefield itself even if victory had been a certainty.

There remains the tantalising possibility that some of the hoard still remains nearby.

We have also surmised (because of the hoard) that Sedlescombe, a Saxon village at the time of the Conquest, was the location of the army's rear HQ, where arriving troops could be formed into units, armed and marched forward to the battle front.

Comparison of Battlefields – Traditional and Blackhorse Hill

Appendix 2 shows the relative strengths of the two locations (Blackhorse Hill and Battle Abbey) as defensive positions. Blackhorse Hill, the overlaid profiles show, has a much greater slope below the estimated shield wall position that the Norman army would have had to scale, than the Battle Abbey site. And the incline to the rear, back into woods, is much lengthier. Blackhorse Hill would have been much more difficult to attack and the ground easier to defend in a fighting withdrawal – all in all Blackhorse Hill was an excellent choice of terrain.

Some accounts have King Harold and Duke William contending for the ground, showing both recognised its value. Harold reached the ground first but only by a few hours and with his army not fully assembled. Troops were arriving after the battle had begun and we can speculate they were marshalled at Sedlescombe (if that was indeed the HQ behind the lines) as they arrived and marched forward as fighting units. Archaeological evidence may one day reveal signs of the Saxon army's presence.

The Route to the Traditional Battlefield (Appendix 3)

Given the short time (less than two hours) that historic accounts say the Norman army had to reach the battlefield and using map plotting and terrain profiling, we show in this appendix that the traditional site could not be reached by the stated battle start time – meaning the battle could not have taken place at the Battle Abbey site.

The Wastings

Appendix 4 shows, using Domesday records, the ravaging of the countryside at and around Hastings. The distribution of 'wastings' indicates that the Norman marauders were operating from a base near the coast in and around Combe Haven providing weight to the old port of Hastings being the site of the Norman camp prior to the battle.

Memorials to the Battle

The naming of geographical features close to the Blackhorse Hill battlefield, shown on the two maps in Appendix 5, through circumstantial evidence indicates that the battle was fought at, or close to those features. We have: Duke's Wood, Bishop's Wood, Red River, Red River Wood, Red River Pond and of course Blackhorse Hill itself. These names can be associated with the battle and Norman leaders taking part in the battle.

Blackhorse Hill is the name given on some maps to our battlefield, while the remaining memorials are in the area where the Saxon rout took place. If the battle took place at Battle Abbey then why are these names so distant from it?

Archaeology

Appendix 6 looks at the archaeology. We recognise that no relevant archaeology has been found at our Blackhorse Hill site, but then as far as is known no one has ever looked. Several sites look promising

SUMMARY OF THE EVIDENCE FOR THE BATTLE SITE

though, including The Mount where King Harold placed his banner before the battle and at the site of the fosse below Blackhorse Hill.

On the other hand, the traditional site has been subjected to intense archaeological scrutiny and nothing has been found and neither is there anything in the Battle Abbey museum to suggest a battle there.

Hastings

Finally, the 1066 battle has always, as far as is known, been called the Battle of Hastings. This has been a puzzle to this writer as the traditional site at Battle Abbey is so distant from Hastings – why not Battle of Crowhurst or Whatlington both of which are much closer? But Hastings makes sense, the Blackhorse Hill site being less than 2 miles from the old port of Hastings. It being named the Battle of Hastings is, in itself, strong evidence for our battle site.

PART III

THE CONQUEST OF ENGLAND

March on Dover
Norman Army's March on London
The Coronation of Duke William
The Crushing of the English Rebellion and Devastation of
the North
Domesday Survey
Death of William

March on Dover

Duke William after his triumph on Blackhorse Hill was in no position to head north and take the capital, so as we have seen, he took the army back to his stronghold (upper and lower forts) beside Combe Haven to lick their wounds, regroup and plan the next moves.

There, *The Carmen* tells us, they remained for a fortnight:

> For a fortnight William remained in camp at the port of Hastings and from there he directed his march towards Dover.[1]

His great victory did not mean William had secured the country. There were unknown numbers of troops still converging on Hastings, although these, learning of the duke's complete victory and Saxon army rout, would no doubt have turned about and headed back the way they had come along with the battle survivors. There were towns and men up and down the country still prepared to fight on. The truth is the Battle of Hastings had been won by a narrow margin against a depleted and tired Saxon army and the duke must have known it. Very seldom in history has a single battle decided the outcome of a war.

No doubt William was using his period of recuperation wisely and, although accounts do not relate it, he might have been dispatching spies to key points across England, particularly the south, to assess the mood of the country and what leaders were remaining with the will and capacity to continue the fight. He probably considered the Saxon army spent, it having lost so many warriors in the three battles (Fulford, Stamford Bridge and now Hastings) fought in the course of the preceding four weeks. William remained cautious until he could gauge relative strengths, morale and intentions, and to receive or plunder supplies and to reinforce his army.

Whether or not William himself accompanied his troops to Dover is not clear from the wording, but more likely the march to Dover was without him, while he sought reinforcements from Normandy and France.

He would have needed more troops as he subdued the country, not only to fight, but to garrison the towns he took on his way to the capital to claim the throne. He would have been looking for reinforcements, and news of his victory spreading through northern France would no doubt have attracted volunteers with promise of land, Saxon land, and of course booty.

The need for more troops, incidentally, belies the claim made in the *Chronicle of Battle Abbey* that William 'burnt the greatest part of his ships'.[2] He would surely have required these to transport them over, making sure they were kept in a good state of repair.

William would have gauged that a direct march on London was unlikely to succeed so, taking in Romney on the way to Dover, he arrived at a 'castle standing on the summit of a steep rock overhanging the sea'.[3] The defenders, considering their position invincible, prepared to fight but capitulated as soon as the duke arrived. Orderic Vitalis tells us the army, or whatever part of it the duke took with him, remained at Dover for eight days, strengthening the ramparts. Leaving the castle garrisoned, he set out for Canterbury where he took the fealty of the men of Kent. Orderic Vitalis, as does *The Carmen*, then has William marching on London where men were gathering in strength preparing to resist.

March on London

The Carmen next has William sending word to Winchester where 'the chief men of the city' were ordered 'to pay tribute as others were doing'. Edith, the dowager queen of King Edward the Confessor who held the city, according to *The Carmen*, ceded it for the sake of peace. This must have been a major blow to those of the remaining ruling class who hoped to organise resistance and defeat William. Some of those, including Stigand the Archbishop of Canterbury, Aeldred Archbishop of York and the Earls of Mercia and Northumbria had declared Edgar the Aethling, grandson of Edmund Ironside, king. Under Edgar, although just a teenager, they hoped to continue the fight to save the country. But in spite of the City of London being in a strong position to hold out behind its massive Roman walls this came to nothing when William's army arrived.

The Carmen tells us the Norman army marched directly on London, where they set up the siege engine 'on the huge mound that has been raised overtops the towers and the ramparts fall, riven by the blows of stones'. It continues 'With many falls in all parts collapse is imminent.' With that, according to *The Carmen*, London capitulated.

Orderic Vitalis tells it slightly differently: the Archbishop of Canterbury with other nobles declared 'Edgar Etheling, son of Edward king of Hungary, son of Edmund Ironside, king, and gave out that they were resolved to fight bravely under their prince.' The duke hearing of this marched on Southwark on the south bank of the Thames at London and, detaching fifty knights, compelled the Saxons who had left the safety of the city to retreat back within the walls with 'many' losses.

The buildings on that side of the Thames were then burnt before the army headed west. Presumably, not feeling strong enough to storm the city, William took his army to Wallingford where, according to Orderic Vitalis, the Archbishop of Canterbury and other nobles met the duke 'and abandoning the cause of Edgar, came to terms with William, to whom they did homage'. The Londoners, we are told, also transferred their allegiance and 'delivered so many hostages as he required', and 'Edgar Etheling, therefore, who had been declared king by the English, … surrendered his person and his kingdom to William.'

Other accounts have this event taking place not at Wallingford but at Berkhamsted north of London.

THE CONQUEST OF ENGLAND

William Crowned King of England

The coronation took place on Christmas Day 1066: 'The day which the world celebrates as the Nativity of Christ, … was at hand; on which feast William determined to wear the crown that he had won and, with the name of the duke renounced, be made king.'[4] The ceremony was conducted by Aeldred, Archbishop of York, the more senior Archbishop of Canterbury, Stigand, having been suspended by Pope Alexander for 'certain crimes'.[5]

The Carmen gives a colourful description of the crown that William 'commanded to be made' which is worth stating:

> He [William] commanded that a noble crown of gold and jewels, such as would be seemly, be fashioned for him by master-craftsmen. … Foremost a ruby adorned the centre of the brow; next after this a radiant jacinth; third in the circlet of wrought gold a topaz glittered; the fourth place a sapphire[6] enriched with beauty; fifth was sardonyx, set at the king's ears, to which chalcedony came next, the sixth in order, seventh was jasper.

There was also a sard, a beryl, an emerald, a chrysoprase, pearl and two amethysts. There is no reason to disbelieve this account, but it must have been no small task to locate these gems and handcraft the crown in the few weeks available. The jeweller also had to fashion a rod and sceptre for the ceremony.

The coronation did not go well. When the assembled English responded in one voice with their assent to William becoming their king in a language William's men-at-arms outside the abbey did not understand, the guards, believing an English rising was taking place, set fire to adjacent houses. The reaction to the supposed uprising is hard to credit, but the result was a scramble by 'men and women of all ranks to escape the church'.

However, the attending bishops 'completed the coronation office with some difficulty, the king himself being much alarmed'. England now had a new king, a Norman king. It had taken over 250 years of Viking attempts (if it is considered that Normans were actually Vikings) on Saxon lands.

Rebellion

William I reigned over England as king, as well as continuing to rule the Duchy of Normandy, for the next twenty-one years. It could not have been an easy time for William, for much of this time he had to contend with rebellion both in England and in his duchy as well as sending expeditions to Brittany to expand his territories. This saw him criss-crossing the Channel throughout his reign to deal with kingly matters or issues in the duchy, as well put down these rebellions, but then this was a way of life for medieval rulers.

It is difficult to assess the amount of time spent on each side of the Channel, but going by the chronology of his travels listed in Chapter 13, it looks as though he spent more time in Normandy than in England. He seems to have trusted his half-brother, Bishop Odo, to rule England during his absences, but Odo's misrule eventually forced William to remove him to prison in Normandy.

William's troubles in England were aggravated by continuing Viking incursions, which had the effect of encouraging English rebellion, even collaboration between the two 'nations'.

One of William's immediate tasks was a programme of castle building, carried out to overawe the inhabitants and from which to suppress them if necessary. The 'White Tower' by the Thames in London is the most famous of these castles.

The first major rebellion occurred at Exeter in 1068, an uprising led by King Harold's mother, Gytha, who hoped to stir Wessex to rise up against Norman rule. This ended in failure. Next, Harold Godwinson's sons, Godwin and Edmund, staged an attack on Bristol with a view to again rousing Wessex to revolt. Perhaps by now the English of the south had had enough of being attacked, especially by Danish invaders.

Next it was the turn of the north: a Danish army arrived by sea in 1069, sailing up the Humber estuary. Allying with Edgar Aethling (who had fled to Scotland) and Walthe, Earl of Huntingdon, they defeated the Normans at York and briefly occupied Northumbria, which at that time consisted of a large swathe of northern England. William responded with overwhelming force and thus began the Normans' 'Harrying of the North', mercilessly pursuing and killing William's enemies, burning settlements and crops and slaughtering animals. At least 100,000 people, it was said, perished of starvation. The north had not recovered from the devastation by Domesday in 1086.

The most well-known 'warrior' holding out against the Normans was Hereward the Wake. Hereward, an Anglo-Danish, East Anglian landowner, operated against the Normans with Danish assistance, in the Fens around Ely. This is a complicated period of English history, but Hereward first appears on the scene in around 1070, looting Peterborough Abbey, claiming it was necessary to pay for weapons and to pay his men. But this did not endear him to the local Saxons and Danish settlers and eventually the Normans launched seaborne attacks and Hereward was paid off in silver to abandon the struggle, such as it was. Remaining resistance in the Fens soon fizzled out and thus ended serious opposition to Norman rule.

Domesday Survey

This survey, well known to those interested in history, was the great administrative act of William's reign. It was, of course, no altruistic exercise but organised to raise taxes, no doubt to pay to strengthen his grip over the country. The survey was ordered at a meeting of nobles at Gloucester in 1085. It is remarkable that the survey was completed by the following year. The survey covered most of the country. Typical data collected were:

- Name of settlement, usually under a named manor, and in which hundred and county it lay.
- Holder or holders of land in 1066 (before conquest) and in 1086.

- Number of households, villagers, small holders, freemen, sokemen, villains and slaves.
- Land area in hides, ploughlands, lord's plough teams, villagers' plough teams.
- Woodland, meadow, pasture, mills (presumably water mills) and fisheries.
- Annual valuation in 1066 (before the conquest) and in 1086 in pounds and shillings.
- How much land area altered between 1066 and 1086.

Death of William

As we have seen in Chapter 13, page 140, William returned to Normandy in 1087, for the last time, to deal with a dispute with the French king, Philip I. William of Malmesbury tells us that William responded to insults from Philip about his belly, which by now had taken on an enormous girth. William of Malmesbury described events:

> Not long after, in the end of the month of August, … collecting an army, he entered France in a hostile manner, trampling down, and laying everything waste: nothing could assuage his irritated mind, so determined was he to revenge this injurious taunt at the expense of multitudes. At last he set fire to the city of Mantes [a town bordering Normandy and France], where the church of St Mary was burnt, together with a recluse who did not think it justifiable to quit her cell even under such an emergency; and the whole property of the citizens was destroyed. Exhilarated by this success, while furiously commanding his people to add fuel to the conflagration, he approached too near the flames.

With the result, William of Malmesbury continues:

> Some say, that his horse leaping over a dangerous ditch, ruptured his rider, where his belly projected over the front of the saddle [the pommel]. Injured by this accident, he

sounded a retreat, and returning to Rouen, as the malady increased he took to his bed. His physicians, when consulted, affirmed, from an inspection of his urine, that death was inevitable.

William expired on 9 September and was interred in the Abbaye-aux-Hommes in Caen aged about 59.

Consequences

The Battle of Hastings was a particularly bloody and uncompromising affair with no mercy shown by either side. Ultimately William had achieved his immediate goal, defeat of the army set on defending their homeland. He had done more than that; the king, the last Saxon king whom William claimed had stolen the crown from him, breaking his solemn pledge to support his legitimate right to the throne bestowed on him by Edward the Confessor, was dead and no longer in the way of his claim.

Following the crowning of William as William I, we have seen that England was not immediately ready to submit to his governance but subsequently the country acquiesced under Norman authoritarian rule. Direct descendants of William ruled England for the next 333 years until the deposition of Richard II, son of the Black Prince. Normans continued to rule Normandy and later Aquitaine, Anjou and Maine as what became known as the Angevin Empire, until lost under King John to King Philip of France, but under Edward III, large swathes of France, including Normandy, were ruled by England following the outbreak of the 100 Years War in 1346 and victories at Crécy and Poitiers. Wales, Scotland and Ireland were also invaded during this time.

The Normans were great builders and had constructed fine castles and cathedrals and churches of stone in Normandy before the Conquest. They continued to do so in England following its occupation, usually replacing simpler Saxon wooden houses of worship with their own larger ones in stone, with cathedrals strengthened with elaborate flying buttresses and other ornate workings. These embellish English cities, towns and countryside; even the numerous castle ruins enhance the English landscape and are popular tourist attractions today. This author has, in particular, the Corfe Castle ruin in Dorset in mind, ruined with gunpower charges under its foundations by Cromwell after its capture from the Royalists in the seventeenth-century Civil War.

And it could be considered a gift that two languages, one Anglo-Saxon, and the other Norman French, could, after coexisting separately side-by-side until the mid-thirteenth century, begin their merger into a common tongue spoken the world over as a preferred working language – it is truly remarkable.

Some sort of feudalism existed in some parts of England prior to the Conquest, though its extent and nature is not too clear (this is a subject we do not need or intend to go into here). But when William took control of England, he enforced feudal law that he had inherited in Normandy. Besides the royal demesnes, he divided England into baronies gifting Saxon lands to his followers and favourites (including churchmen) in exchange for payments and other obligations, especially the requirement to provide levies in time of war. These great landholders shared out a large part of their lands to other Normans and Frenchmen, often knights, who in turn owed the same obligations to their baron. At the bottom were the Saxon (and perhaps Danish) peasantry, many of whom would have had their own holdings before the Conquest. The peasantry (serfs) in exchange for labour and sometimes military service for the lord of the manor (as the knights often came to be known, with their manor houses and associated lands) were allowed use of land for cultivation of crops and rearing sheep and cattle.

It was to be another three centuries before England and Englishness were gradually able to reassert themselves and even longer for the phasing out of the feudal system. The eventual merging of Saxon and Norman cultures saw the evolution of a more united and resilient society, taking a respected place in a Europe of nations, yet powerful enough to avert invasion for the next thousand years. The avoidance of further incursions and social disruption has no doubt contributed to the relative stability enjoyed over this long period of time.

However, Sir Tony Robinson (broadcaster, particularly on archaeological digs) while recognising this, considered that there has been a lasting divide in society as a result of the Conquest, succinctly, although perhaps provocatively, asserting:

> It also gave us a new aristocratic elite who spoke a different language and were completely cut off from the people they were ruling and a thousand years later that social gulf is still taking a long time to bridge.

The Saxon defeat on Blackhorse Hill changed nearly everything.

Bibliography/Sources

Abels, Ricard, *English Logistics and Military Administration; 871–1066 and Impact of Viking Wars*, www.acedemia.edu, published 2012

Baudri, abbott of the monastery of Saint-Pierre (Bourgueil, Loire), Bishop of Dol-de-Bretagne, *Adelae Comitissa*, early 12th century

Bishop Odo, half-brother of William the Conqueror (thought to have commissioned the tapestry), *Bayeux Tapestry*, Bayeux Museum, Bayeux, France. Possibly embroidered by English embroiderers in the years soon after the Norman Conquest

Blair, Peter, *An Introduction to Anglo-Saxon England, second edition*, Cambridge University Press, 1977

Florence of Worcester (principal author), *Chronicon ex chronicis*, manuscript compiled 1141, translated by Benjamin Thorpe (1780–1870), publisher unknown

Gaimar, Geoffrey, *L'Estoire des Engleis* (*The History of the English*), manuscript compiled 12th century

Guy, Bishop of Amiens (attributed to), *The Carmen de Hastingae Proelio (Song of the Battle of Hastings)*, manuscript compiled soon after the Norman Conquest, Latin to English translation by Catherine Morton and Hope Muntz, Clarendon Press (OUP), 1972

Henry of Huntingdon, *Historia Anglorum*, original manuscript 1154, Latin to English translation by Diana Greenway, Clarendon Press (OUP) 1996

Lawson, Michael, *Battle of Hastings,* believed to be self-published, first print 2002

Mais, Petre, *The Land of Cinque Ports,* publisher unknown, 1949

Monk of Battle Abbey, *Brevis Relatio de Guillelmo nobilissimo comite Normannorum (Brief History of the most-noble William, Count* [duke] *of the Normans)*, original manuscript 12th century, Cambridge University Press

Monks of Battle Abbey, *Chronicle of Battel Abbey*, original manuscript compiled mid-12th century, Latin to English translation by Mark Anthony Lower, publisher of English translation J.R. Smith, 1851

Orderic Vitalis, Benedictine monk and English Chronicler, *Historia Ecclesiastica*, first Latin compilation in printed book by Adam de Breme, 1579

Searle, Eleanor, *Battle Abbey Exemptions: The Forged Charters*, Oxford University Press, paper published 1968

Unknown scribes, *Anglo-Saxon Chronicle, History of the Anglo-Saxons from Late 9th Century,* compiled 9th to 12th century

Vincent, Alex, *Roman Roads of Sussex*, Middleton Press, July 2000

Wace (Master), medieval Norman poet, *Roman de Rou (History of Rollo)*, William Pickering, 1837

William I, King, commissioned by the king and compiled by the king's officials, *Domesday Book,* manuscript 1867

William of Jumièges (monk) and contemporary of Battle of Hastings, English translation by Elisabeth van Houts, *Gesta Normannorum Ducum*; manuscript compiled about 1070, Clarendon Press (OUP), 1992

William of Malmesbury, *Gesta Regum Anglorum (Deeds of English Kings) AD 449–1127*; published manuscript compiled 1127, English translation J.A. Giles, 1847

William of Poitiers, *Gesta Guillelmi*, manuscript compiled soon after Norman Conquest. English translation by R. David and Marjorie Chibnall, Clarendon Press (OUP), 1998

Notes

Acknowledgements

1. To locate this feature, refer to Figure 2.15.

Chapter 1: Battle of Hastings – Greater Battlefield Topography

1. The French army at Azincourt in 1415 was not only prevented from properly deploying by the woods on either side of the battle at Azincourt and Tramevin but the woods acted as a very effective flank guard for the much smaller English force.
2. Second edition.
3. Method of applying electrical energy to the ground to detect irregularities below the surface. In archaeology used to find evidence of artefacts and building remains not evident at the surface.
4. lidar: acronym for 'light detection and ranging' technology; ground imaging often taken from aircraft.
5. OS map 124 for Hastings and Bexhill, reference: TQ778103.
6. Refer to OS map for identification of this feature in Figure 3.1.
7. This works out at a density of fifty-eight men and eight horses, plus supplies, per acre.
8. This writer acknowledges the article written by Jean Taylor that appeared in the Winter 1973 (issue No.34) edition of the *Kent Archaeological Review* and is grateful for the authorisation granted to use it here (the article was based on the work of Henry F. Cleere).

9. Beauport Park was named after the village of Beauport near Quebec, Canada, by General Sir James Murray who was second in command under General Wolfe at the battle of Quebec in 1759.

Chapter 2: The Saxon Port of Hastings and Norman Pre-Battle Camp

1. This book recognises the French do not consider it to be entirely English-owned and know it by its more neutral name – La Manche, named after the waterway's shape, that of a sleeve.
2. Second edition.
3. See: https://www.oldenglishtranslator.co.uk
4. Using the online 'Old English to Modern English Translator', the translation of the word, 'hill' in the *Chronicle of Battle Abbey* produced no useful outcome; so we tried 'ridge', not unlike the terrain in question.
5. Roman artefacts have been found in the area.
6. Hastings burh (Chapel Field) area calculation:
Aspect ratio of field: $b/a = 4.5/6.5 = 0.692$
Perimeter of field; $2(a+b) = 2,000$ft
$a + 0.692a = 1,000$ft
$\qquad a = 1,000/1.692$ft
$\qquad\ \ = 591$ft making b 409ft
Area of burh $a \times b = 241,719$ft^2 or 5.5 acres with 43,560ft^2 to the acre
7. http://www.secretsofthenormaninvasion.com/part54.htm
8. Refer to Richard Abels' 2012 paper published in Academia.edu: 'English Logistics and military administration, page 871, – '1066: The Impact of the Viking Wars'.

Chapter 3: Saxon and Norman Strategic Considerations

1. William of Malmesbury's account says that three propositions were offered Harold: 'either that Harold should relinquish the kingdom according to agreement', [meaning, supposedly, the agreement Harold may have made under duress when he visited Normandy in

NOTES

1064], 'or hold it of William [as a suzerain]; or decide the matter by single combat in the sight of either army'.
2. *The Carmen* (refer to Bibliography) was written by the Bishop of Amiens – excusing this act, blaming the people, currying favour with Duke William.
3. *The Carmen* is currying favour with William, here excusing this act by blaming the people for their perfidy.

Chapter 4: Did the Normans Land at Pevensey or Hastings?

1. Meaning in this context, anything written over the past two centuries.
2. One of the earliest authors, E.A. Freeman, writes (1854): 'William of Normandy landed without opposition at Pevensey' without again referring to it, leaving the reader with the impression that was the starting out point of the army. M.K. Lawson has the Malfosse incident taking place after the main battle. That is at the Battle Abbey battlesite.
3. In fact the crossing, as it was, was not without mishap, Wace recording that one of the sailors was drowned, 'being in one of the lost ships'.
4. *The Chronicle of Florence of Worcester* relates that provisions failing towards the time of the Nativity of St Mary [8 September], both fleet and army were disbanded.
5. Wace has it from his father as 'seven hundred less four' and William of Jumiege's 3,000 ships, discredited.
6. Probably one retelling the story of the other.
7. From William of Jumièges' account. Romney at the time of these events was a coastal Cinque Port on a vast haven more extensive than that at Hastings and now nearly 3 miles from the sea cut off by the constant eastward drift of sand and shingle.
8. The feast itself being on Saturday, 30 October.
9. *The Carmen* does not actually name the first landing place or even the date.
10. About 9 o'clock.
11. Halley's Comet.
12. With all this traffic along the East Sussex and Kent coast it is not surprising Wace understood the fleet made its first landfall at Hastings.

Chapter 5: How was the Fleet Disposed after Landing?

1. Combe is a narrow valley or deep hollow, especially one enclosed on all but one side. So Combe Haven would be the same but filled with water. The etymology of the word 'Combe' is a survival, mainly from an Old English place name and probably a British word derived from a Celtic base. So Combe Haven could have been the name in use at the time of the Conquest adding weight to the findings in Chapter 1, that Hastings Port was in the Combe Haven.
2. We have to be careful here; Wace is our source for the number of vessels: 'I heard my father say – although I was but a lad – that there were seven hundred ships, less four [696], when they sailed from St Valeri'. In addition, Wace says there were other smaller vessels for transport. He says he had heard (but did not know whether it was true) that altogether there were 3,000 vessels. Historian's discount the higher figure and generally settle for 700 ships.
3. We have seen Wace's account has 'each ship ranged side by side'.

Chapter 6: Erecting the Upper and Lower Forts at Hastings

1. A large part of which no longer exist following the construction of the A2690, Bexhill link road, in 2016.
2. *The Carmen.*
3. A field called 'Five Acre field' in the book.
4. It is interesting to consider where loyalties may have lain amongst any Normans still in England at the time of the Conquest.
5. Wace relates the carpenters, who came after, 'had great axes in their hands, and planes and adzes hung at their sides', all tools for woodworking.

Chapter 7: King Harold Selects his Battlefield – The Highest Hill

1. Blackhorse Hill is at the highest point of the hill by the A2100 road at spot height 141m. *The Carmen de Hastingae Proelio* (line 375),

is the evidence that before battle King Harold set his banner on the heights of Blackhorse Hill, Telham Ridge: '*In summo montis uexillum uertice fixit, Affigique iubet cetera signa sibi.*' [On the highest point of the summit he planted his banner.]
2. Refer to Chapter 1 for Margery's map of Roman road routings in the South-East.
3. Wace, writing in the twelfth century, had no reason to challenge the tradition by then well-established of the battlefield and abbey site being co-located; though he did write that the assertion that the high altar stood on the spot where Harold was killed was a mere assertion invented by the monks (source of the quote still pending).

Chapter 8: The Normans March to Battle

1. What William means in effect is that if Harold admits William as the rightful king, he will allow Harold to retain his extensive estates.
2. Meaning that William is not recognising the legitimacy of the title to the fief held by Harold.
3. Wace writes that William gave the spies food. If this was so, there would not have been time to consume it at the Norman camp.
4. Time taken distance (miles) divided by speed (mph).
5. The distance to the traditional Battle Abbey battlefield is just too far for an army to have reached it in time – see Appendix 3.

Chapter 9: The Battle

1. Equivalent to mathematical proof by induction, you might say.
2. Apart from the pioneering work of Nick Austin.
3. Some writers have even given way to defeatism, admitting to the impossibility of giving any straightforward account of the Battle of Hastings. And Eleanor Searle in a footnote to her translation of the description of the Malfosse incident in the *Chronicle of Battle Abbey* (Oxford Medieval Texts, Clarendon Press, 1980), writes: 'I have taken some pains to ascertain the locality of this shocking incident, but can find no place which, in the ordinary use of language, can be called a "dreadful precipice".' She was, it seems, like many authors

writing about the Battle of Hastings, unable to match the topography with the historic description, but unwilling to contemplate the possibility that the battle might have occurred somewhere else.
4. Some contemporary accounts have the defensive position on Blackhorse Hill contested by the Normans as Harold was occupying it. If so, it could not have been by the main army marching up from Hastings defences and may have been an advanced contingent or even forces that had been ordered up overnight from Pevensey's left flank. This is speculation and there is no certainty that occupation of the hill defences was contested.
5. Ibid – see previous page.
6. Refer to William of Poitiers' account, see Chapter 8: 'the duke with his men climbed slowly up the steep slope'. There is no steep slope at the Battle Abbey site to match that described in this chapter and described by William of Poitiers.
7. Some believe that cross-bows were no longer used after the fall of the 'Western Empire' in AD 476 and only reappeared at the time of the First Crusade – refer to Catherine Morton and Hope Muntz's Oxford Medieval Texts' version of *The Carmen*.
8. See Appendix 1 for an understanding of the role of Sedlescombe in the Saxon battle plan.
9. See Figure 9.6. (Photograph of slope at Crowhurst chalet park taken from below, August 2020).
10. Wace.
11. The damage makes it sound more like a bill, the long-handled bill, than a hatchet.
12. Henry of Huntingdon. Some translations have 'covered' instead of 'concealed'.
13. That is the deep valley to the west of the defended heights.
14. See *The Carmen* – line.373/4: 'Preparing to meet the enemy the king mounted the hill and strengthened both his wings with noble men.'
15. Harold had his own fleet to prevent a losing Norman army returning to Normandy as told in various accounts including the *Anglo-Saxon Chronicle*: 'And that same year that he became king, he went out with a fleet against William …'
16. Refer to Note 3 in this Chapter regarding Eleanor Searle's inability to find the 'dreadful precipice'.

NOTES

17. William of Malmesbury (*Gesta Regum Anglorum*), booke III, Section 277.
18. Wace.

Chapter 10: Rout

1. No doubt meaning one of the gullies.
2. This writer crossing the area from west to east in 2020, in good weather, needed three hours to traverse less than a mile of this forest.
3. Now Beaufort Park.
4. Appendix 5 deals with this in greater detail.

Chapter 11: The Mount

1. At OS Explorer 124, map reference 57763/11411.
2. A magnifying glass is needed to see it.
3. Neither is it named on the current 1:50,000 map.
4. After much local enquiry.
5. By Sheldon Blakeman, New York.
6. The British Library catalogue for 1880 takes four pages to list his works.
7. Refer to Chapter 2: Identifying the Anglo-Saxon Port of Hastings – the Road to Hastings, for the discussion of the route of the road from the port to the bloomery.
8. Next to the water tower on the A2100 road.

Chapter 12: Burials

1. If so, it would be consistent with Norman (Norseman) heritage.

Chapter 13: The Battlefield that wasn't

1. Eleanor Searle in her translation (Oxford Medieval Texts: Clarendon Press 1980), does not regard the *Chronicle of Battle Abbey* to be a

chronicle as such, but is more of a defence of ecclesiastical and secular rights.
2. John Grehan, together with Martin Mace have published their history in 2012: *The Battle of Hastings the Uncomfortable Truth*.
3. YouTube interview given at the town of Battle, 13 December 2013.
4. *The English Historical Review*, Vol.83, No.328 (July, 1968), pp. 449–480, published by Oxford University Press.
5. Ibid – previous page.
6. 'that the abbey of Battle should be entirely free from all subjection of bishops as Christ Church, Canterbury'.
7. The *Chronicle* claims that a monk named Faber (Latin for Smith) from Marmoutier, France heard the vow proclaimed.
8. The *Chronicle*, Page 10.
9. Freeman 1894.
10. Until Thomas Beckett.
11. British Museum.
12. On the evidence of the *Chronicle of Battle Abbey*.
13. Searle does not say so, but presumably this was a peculiarity of the time of forging.
14. Demonstrated by Mr Bishop and Mr Chaplais.

Appendix 1 – The Sedlescombe Hoard

1. The British Museum has some of the hoard in its collection of Anglo-Saxon coinage.
2. Dolley calls this: 'Inventory 327'.
3. Mark Lower was a founder of Sussex Archaeological Society.
4. Wace.

Appendix 2 – Comparison of Traditional Battlefield with that at Blackhorse Hill

1. The battle area three-dimensional scale model, Figures 1.1 and 1.2. Chapter 1 allows of the two competing sites' visualisation and comparison from every angle.

NOTES

Appendix 5 – Memorials

1. No known archaeological investigations have been conducted at the Blackhorse Hill battle site and metal detecting in the area is discouraged.
2. Located just north of the Black Horse public house, Telham.

Appendix 6 – Archaeology

1. English Heritage is wholly controlled by Historic England, a body corporate established under National Heritage Act 1983 and is an Executive Non-Departmental Public Body sponsored by the Department for Digital, Culture, Media and Sports.
2. At the time of writing, Channel 4 is a statutory corporation, without shareholders established under the terms of the Broadcasting Act 1990.
3. Chapter 13 discusses reasons the monks of Battle Abbey had motives for 'stating that' and the reasons for it.
4. One of Sir Tony Robinson's summarising remarks.

Appendix 7 – Senlac

1. Eleanor Searle in her translation of *The Chronicle of Battle Abbey*, writes in a footnote to the *Chronicle*'s 'the field being covered in dead bodies': 'The Conqueror is said to have given one portion of the field of battle the name Sanguelac, or the lake of blood', though she does not give the provenance of the name.

PART III – The Conquest of England

1. From *The Carmen* account, line 598.
2. The toll on William's troops did not end with the battle, for instance Orderic Vitalis tells of Norman losses to illness: 'While he [William] lay there [Dover] a great number of soldiers, who devoured flesh-meat half raw and drank too much water, died of dysentery.' These

additional losses show, surely, that William could not possibly have continued with his subjugation of England and the march on London without substantial reinforcements from the continent. For this he would have needed as many vessels as possible. Being the good planner he was, he must have anticipated this before he set out from Normandy. He would not have burned his boats.

3. Ibid Chapter 6
4. *The Carmen* (line 623) says William remained at Dover for a month.
5. *The Carmen*, line 753.
6. The sapphire in the State Crown at the Tower of London is said to have been worn in the coronation ring of Edward the Confessor in 1042. It was removed, it is thought, when Edward was reburied in 1163, but could it have been taken in 1066 to be mounted in William the Conqueror's crown for his coronation?

Index

A21 (road), 75
A2100 (road), 28, 48, 49, 125, 127–9, 156, 169–70, 192, 195
A2690 link road, vii, 40, 192
Abbaye-aux-Hommes, Caen, 183
Abbey Museum, Battle, 159, 173
Aeldred, Archbishop of York, 178–9
Alfred the Great, 7–11, 14, 67
Anglo-Norman franchises, 137
Anglo-Saxon Chronicle, 2, 58, 64, 68, 166, 194
Apulia, 86
Archbishop of Rouen, 17
Archbishop Theobald, 138
Arthur, William, MA Etymologist, 126–7
astronomical twilight, 85
Athelstan, 8, 10–11, 13–14
Austin, Nick, vii, x, 26, 31, 33, 36–8, 40, 47–9, 54, 66–7, 73, 133, 137, 155, 160, 193

Barnby, Erika, author's daughter, ix
Barnby, Francine, author's wife, ix
Battle Abbey, x, xv, 28, 36, 55–6, 62, 72–3, 77, 87–90, 97, 103, 111, 127, 134–7, 139, 141, 143–4, 147, 149–53, 156, 159, 160–62, 171–3, 191, 193–4, 197
account, 62, 73, 90
estate purchased for the nation, 134
Baudri of Bourgeuil, 100–101
Bayeux
Cathedral, 18
Tapestry, vii, ix, x, 18, 62, 65, 70, 106, 109, 114, 116, 131, 156, 167
Beauport
bloomery, 47, 84
Park, xii, 28, 47, 49, 76, 92, 119–21, 123, 156, 167, 169, 190
Wood, xii, 27, 29, 48–9, 75, 93, 117, 123, 125, 133, 158, 161, 165, 169
Benedictine monastery, 135
Bishop's Wood, 27, 156, 172
Blackhorse Hill, vi, vii, viii, x, xi, xii, xv, 22, 25, 27–8, 47, 49, 77–8, 83–5, 88, 92, 95, 97–103, 108, 112, 114, 120, 123, 125, 127–9, 134–5, 142, 146, 149, 150–51, 156, 157, 161, 164, 167–73, 176, 186, 192–4, 196–7

Bosham, 18, 131–2
  Holy Trinity Church, 131
Boyer, Abel, 126–7
Brede Levels, 119
Bretons, 18–19, 86, 102, 105, 112, 140
British Numismatic Society publication, 146
Browne, Sir Anthony, King's Master of Horse, 135
Brunanburh, Battle of, 11
Bulverhythe
  Island, 24
  Road, xiii
  village, 42, 45, 60, 128
Bury St Edmunds, 6

Caldbec Hill, 137, 160
Canterbury, 31, 177
Canute (*also* King Cnut), 13–14, 33
Carmen, The, 53–4, 58, 62–3, 65, 71–2, 75, 81, 83, 85, 92, 95, 97, 99, 104–105, 110, 115–117, 130–33, 164, 166–7, 170, 176–9, 191–2, 194, 197–9
Chapel Field, 37–40, 67, 190
Chichester Cathedral, 137–8
Chronicle of Battle Abbey, xiv, 34–6, 58, 62–3, 65, 70, 89, 110, 134, 136–40, 142–3, 158, 165, 177, 190, 193, 195–7
Cinque Ports, 32–3, 66
civil twilight, 85
Cockley Cley, 44–5
Coin of William I reign, 163
Colchester, hearing, 138
Combe Haven, vii, viii, x, xiii, 7, 22, 24, 26–8, 33, 36–8, 40, 43, 47, 54, 56, 58, 60–1, 63, 66–7, 69, 73, 80, 83, 88, 90, 101, 120, 152, 155, 164–6, 172, 176, 192
Count of Boulogne, 56
comparing the topography, xvi, 22, 59, 77, 89–90, 101–102, 123, 167, 189, 194
comparison of battlefields, 22, 45, 149, 171, 196
Croix pattée (Christian Cross on the Conqueror's coin), 163, 170
Crowhurst
  Park, viii, 47, 97–8, 129, 194
  village, 77, 133, 160

Danish attack, 141
Dempster, Roger, viii
dismantled forts, 53, 63, 67, 166
Dissolution of the Monasteries, 135
Domesday
  Book, 64, 144, 155, 172
  Survey, 175, 181
Dover, 15, 32, 50, 75, 146, 155, 175–7, 197–8
Drigswell, 155
Duke's Wood, 27, 156, 172

East Lexham, 43–4
Edgar (the) Aethling, 178, 181
Edmund Ironside, 13–14, 178
Edmund of East Anglia, King, (Edmund the Martyr), 6
Edward the Confessor, King, xv, 14, 17, 19, 33, 51, 56, 69, 82, 146, 148, 170, 177, 184, 198
Edward the Elder, 10
English fleet, 51

INDEX

English Heritage, 134–5, 159–60, 197
Erik the Red, 5
Ethelred the Unready, King, 7, 13–14
Eu, Earl of, (Walter Fitz Lambert), 147
Eustace of Pontieu, 116

Faber, William, monk, 140
Feast of St. Michael, 58
Florence of Worcester, 57, 95, 101, 191
fosse, 63, 67, 76, 96–7, 99, 101, 108, 111–113, 168–9, 173

Gesta Regum Anglorum, 195
Giffard, 116
Godwin family, the, 14–15
  Earl, 15, 147
gonfanons, 87
Google Earth (GE) satellite imaging, xvi, 26, 41, 45, 90, 165
greater battlefield, viii, 22–4, 125, 137, 189
Grehan, John, 136, 160, 196
ground radar, 133, 159
ground resistivity surveys, 66
Gurth, 87, *See also* Gyrth
Guthrum, 8–9,
Guy of Burgundy, 17
Gyrth, 15, 114
Gytha, Mother of Harold II, 180

Haesten, 9
Hakon, 19
Halfdan (Halfdene) Ragnarsson, 6–7

Harald Hardrada, King of Norway, 51–2, 74, 79
Hardicanute (*also* Harthacnut), 14, 33
Harold Godwinson, Earl, 19, 51, 180 *see also*: Harold II, King of England
Harold II, King of England, v, vii, x, 14–15, 18, 19, 25, 27, 32, 48–9, 51–5, 57, 61, 63, 67, 69, 70–71, 74–9, 81–3, 86–7, 92, 95–9, 102–103, 106–108, 110–112, 114–118, 122–3, 128, 131–2, 134–6, 146–7, 149–50, 160, 165–7, 170–71, 173, 180, 190, 193–4
  death of, 105, 115–116, 118, 135, 193
  interment of, 131–2
Hasketon, 45
Hastingas tribe, 34
Hastings
  Cinque Port of, vii, xiii
  Old, 26–7, 32–3, 42–3, 47, 67
  Port of, viii, x, 26–8, 31–6, 40–41, 45–47, 49–50, 54, 57, 67, 155, 160, 156–6, 172–3, 190, 195
  railway line to London, vii
Hazelhurst, 155
Hechelande (*also spelt* Hechland & Hechlande in documents), 34–6, 63, 68, 136, 165
Henry I, King of England, 144
Henry II, King of England, 138, 143–4
Henry VIII, King of England, 135
Henry I, King of France, 17

201

Henry of Huntingdon, 14, 58, 74, 76, 96, 108, 194
Hereward the Wake, 181
highest point of the summit, 74, 99, 128, 167, 169, 192–3
Hilary, Bishop, 138
Hythe, 32

iron oxide, 161
Isle of Wight, 141

Julius Caesar, 27, 57

Kent Street, viii, 27, 49, 123, 146, 158

Lawson, Michael, 66, 191
Leftwich, John, viii
Leofwine, 15, 114
Lidar, 26, 66, 160, 189,
Lindisfarne (Holy Island), 2–4
London, 9–10, 27, 31, 50, 57, 106, 118, 123, 146, 155, 178
    Tower of, 180, 198
Longships, 27, 53, 55, 62–3, 70–71
Lower, Mark Anthony, 35, 146

Maine, 86
Malfosse, 95, 107, 109–12, 161, 191, 193
Maldon, Battle of, 13
Margery, Ivan, 29, 75, 193
Marmoutier, 140, 142, 196
Matilda, wife of William I, death of, 141
Memorials, 123, 157, 172, 197
'Michaelmass' day, 58
misrule of England, 141

Monkham Wood, 26
Montague, Sixth Viscount, 135
Montjoie/Mountjoy 126–7
Mount, The, vi, 48, 114, 125–30, 156, 161, 163, 167, 169–70, 173, 195

Napoleonic Wars, 126, 170
nautical twilight, 85
Non-ferrous artefacts, 161
Norman
    archers, 55, 105
    camp, vii, 27–8, 35, 81, 83, 87–8, 172, 193
    French, 13, 185
    helmet, 160
    pre-battle activities, 80
Numismatic Chronicle, 146

Odo, Bishop, 18, 70–71, 140–41, 156–7, 180
Old English, xv, 34–5, 190, 192
Orderic Vitalis, 20, 81, 97, 112, 119, 162, 169, 177–8, 197

Peterborough Abbey, 181
Pevensey, 26, 34, 55–9, 62, 63, 68, 155, 166, 191, 194
Piddinghoe, 41, 43, 45
Porter, Roy, 160
prefabricated fort, 67, 70, 72, 166–7
pre-Hastings battle parley, 52, 81, 83

Ragnar Lodrok, 5–6
Ralph the Timid, (Earl of Hereford), 56

INDEX

Redgeland Wood (*also known* as Hrycglande) vii, 27, 36, 63, 68–9, 74, 165
Red River, 27, 158, 162, 172
resistance to Norman Rule, 181
restored dismantled fort, 71
River Brede, 28
Robert of Jumièges, 15
Robert the Devil, 13
Rollo, 12
Roman
    bloomery, xii, 28, 47–9, 75–6, 128, 165, 195 *see also* Beauport Wood bloomery
    fortress, 55
    old Roman road, 27, 84, 147–7
    to London, 155
Romney, 32, 57, 62, 177, 191

St Claire sur Epte, Treaty of, 12
St Martin, monastery of, 134
St Sussane, siege of, 141
St Valery (-sur-Somme), 20, 32, 50–51, 56
Sandwich, 32
Saxon
    burh, vii, 27, 36–8, 49–50, 67, 72, 90, 165–7
    fleet, 53, 57
    line, 77, 104–106, 150
    Shield Wall, 27–8, 100, 110, 127, 166
Searle, Eleanor, 137–9, 143–4, 193–7
Sedlescombe
    Hoard, 146, 170, 196
    village, viii, 30–31, 106, 147–8, 171, 194, 196

Seffrid, Bishop of Chichester, 144
Senlac, 162, 197
Sicily, 86
Sihtric of York, 11
Sir Tony Robinson, 159, 186, 197
Southease, 43, 45
Southwark, 178
Spanish Armada, 126, 170
Stamford Bridge (and Battle of), 50–51, 53, 69, 74, 78, 98, 123, 141, 146–7, 161, 176
Stephen, King of England (Stephen of Blois), 138, 143
Stigand, Archbishop of Canterbury, 178–9
Sweyn Forkbeard, 13

Taillefer (a juggler), 103–104, 106
Telham
    escarpment, 27, 98, 156
    Ridge, 114, 128, 135, 146, 161, 193
    village, 75, 197
Time Team, 159–60
Tostig, 15, 51
Tucker, John, viii, 46

Uffington White Horse, 7
upper fort, 36, 67, 71, 85, 166–8
Upper Wilting Farm, 27, 36–7, 39, 69, 73, 165

Vexin, The, border dispute in, 141
Vincent, Alex, viii

Wace, 52, 57–9, 63, 67–8, 71, 73, 76, 81–2, 84, 86–7, 96–100,

102–103, 105–108, 113–118, 122, 131–2, 164, 166–9, 191–6
Walter de Luci, Abbot, 138
Waltham Abbey, 131–2
Walthe, Earl of Huntingdon, 181
Wastings, The, 64, 172
Watling Street, 8, 75, 146
Weald, 28–9, 31, 75
Webster family, 134
Wedmore, Treaty of, 8, 12
Welsh campaigns, 141
West Hill, Norman castle, 59
William I, King of England, xv, 139, 143–4, 180, 184
    Christmas Day coronation, xv, 179
    promise to found a suitable free Monastery, 136–7
William Fitz Osbern, 143
William of Jumièges, 17, 56–7, 68, 73, 191
William of Malmesbury, 11, 80, 108–109, 134–5, 182, 190, 195
William of Poitiers, xi, 57, 62, 72, 87–8, 95, 97, 102, 108, 113, 116, 168, 194
Wilting camp, 78, 87
Wilting Farm, vii, 37–8, 40, 49, 66–7, 73, 80, 84, 152–3, 166–7
Winchester, 7, 10, 14, 31, 38, 177
Wulfnorth, 19